ALL ABOUT
MUSIC THEORY

A FUN AND SIMPLE GUIDE TO UNDERSTANDING MUSIC

SPECIAL CD INCLUDES 90 TRACKS OF YO...

W9-BVS-642

by Mark Harrison

II-V-I Progression in Major Keys

Cmaj 7

C 6

G 7

I or I

Dm 7

IV

II-V-I Progression in Minor Keys

CmMaj 7 Cm 6 Cm 7

G 7 (b9)

I or I
(jazz)

I
(pop/commercial)

Dm 7 (b5)

V

Combining II-V-I Progressions from Major and Minor Keys

Gmaj 7

D 7

Am 7

VI

II

Bz

F#m 7 (b5)

Tritone Substitutions for

ISBN 978-1-4234-5208-9

HAL•LEONARD® CORPORATION

7777 W. BLUEMOUND RD. P.O. BOX 13819 MILWAUKEE, WI 53213

Visit Hal Leonard Online at
www.halleonard.com

ABOUT THE AUTHOR

Mark Harrison studied classical piano as a child, and by his teenage years was playing in various rock bands in his native Southern England. In the 1980s he began writing music for TV and commercials, including a piece that was used for British Labor Party ads in a national election. He also appeared on British television (BBC) and became a fixture on London's pub-rock circuit.

In 1987 he relocated to Los Angeles to experience the music business in the U.S. He soon began performing with top musicians such as John Molo (Bruce Hornsby band), Jay Graydon (Steely Dan), Jimmy Haslip (Yellowjackets), and numerous others. Mark currently performs with his own contemporary jazz band (Mark Harrison Quintet), as well as with the popular Steely Dan tribute band Doctor Wu.

Mark continues to write music for television and his recent credits include *Saturday Night Live*, *The Montel Williams Show*, *American Justice*, *Celebrity Profiles*, *America's Most Wanted*, *True Hollywood Stories*, the British documentary program *Panorama*, among many others.

Mark has also become one of the top contemporary music educators in Los Angeles. He taught at the renowned Dick Grove School of Music for six years, instructing hundreds of musicians from all around the world. Mark currently runs a busy private teaching studio, catering to the needs of professional and aspiring musicians alike. His students include Grammy-winners, hit songwriters, members of the Boston Pops and Los Angeles Philharmonic, and first-call touring musicians with major acts.

Mark's music instruction books are used by thousands of musicians in over twenty countries and are recommended by the Berklee College of Music for all their new students. He has also written "Master Class" articles for *Keyboard* and *How To Jam* magazines, covering a variety of different keyboard styles and topics.

You're welcome to visit Mark at *www.harrisonmusic.com*, where you'll find information about his educational products and services, as well as his live performance activities and schedule.

BRIEF CONTENTS

FULL CONTENTS

INTRODUCTION

ABOUT THIS BOOK

Welcome to *All About Music Theory*. This book is designed to help you understand how music works, whether you are a beginner, a more experienced musician, or an enthusiast who just wants to know more about the music you hear on the radio. You may be asking yourself: "Why do I need music theory anyway?" Well, the fact that you've opened this book suggests that you're at least a little bit curious! I firmly believe that every musician needs to know at least some music theory, and if you enjoy listening to music you'll appreciate it much more if you know something about what's going on "under the hood," so to speak!

One complaint I hear a lot from musicians and students is that music theory courses (whether taken in college or done on a self-study basis) are often boring and do not relate to their musical needs. Well, I've done my best to make this book both entertaining and informative, whether your interests run to classical music or rock 'n' roll (or both). For example, if you're interested in playing classical piano, we'll show you how music notation works so that you can read notes on the staff. On the other hand, if you're a guitar player wanting to write your own rock songs, we'll show you how chords are created and then combined into progressions... as well as lots of other cool stuff!

Knowledge of music theory will help you express and develop your musical ideas. For instance, theory will help you choose chords to go with a melody line, and show you how to voice the chords to fit the musical style. Now we all know some musicians with great ears who can improvise all this stuff on the spot, and these people inspire us to do better with our own music. Well, the theory examples in this book will probably show you some aspects of music (melodies, rhythms, chords, and so on) that are new to your ears—so working on these examples will get these sounds "in your ears," and thereby extend what you are able to do musically. In this way, music theory and "playing by ear" will reinforce and support one another, and that's when the theory becomes fun and productive.

Music theory can also help you communicate with other musicians. For instance, if you want your musician friends to play the new song you've written, you'll be able to teach them the song much more easily if you can describe the chords (as in, "Nigel, can you play a C7 chord here?") and the form (as in, "Hey guys, the intro lasts for eight bars, and then we go to the verse.").

Here are some different ways you can use this book:

- as a theory method or teaching aid if you are a beginning-level singer, instrumentalist, or songwriter;
- as a theory reference to "fill in the gaps" if you are a more experienced player, or if you "play by ear";
- as a way to learn more about music in general, and how its different elements fit together.

Throughout this book we have notated musical examples for different instruments: Piano, guitar, bass, and drums. Most of the examples can be adapted to fit any instrument. If you don't have an instrument, you can still sing along to many of the examples. Even if your primary goal is not to become an instrumentalist, consider buying an inexpensive portable keyboard (or guitar) to play the examples as you are learning them; this certainly will help to get the sounds "in your ears."

This book is divided into different sections or parts. You can work through from beginning to end, or you can just jump into any section you wish. You can easily review material from an earlier section as necessary.

Section 1: Basic Theory 101 gets you started with reading and writing music, and shows you where the notes are located on the piano and guitar. We'll learn how different rhythms are notated, how music is organized into measures with time signatures, how to create major scales, and how to read and write *key signatures* (those pesky sharps or flats that you see at the beginning of the music). After that we'll see how intervals are used to create melodies, and how simple *chords* (triads) are built and combined into progressions.

Section 2: Beyond the Basics introduces you to some more scales (modal, pentatonic, and blues) and demonstrates how these scales are essential elements in different musical styles. This section also covers minor scales and keys, as well as more advanced time signatures and rhythms. We'll also learn how to build four-part (seventh) chords and combine them into progressions. Finally, we'll see how harmony (chord progressions) and counterpoint ideas can be added to a melody.

Section 3: Intermediate Stuff then delves into five-part (ninth) chords and their alterations, which are essential elements in jazz and R&B styles. We'll derive the most fundamental chord progression in jazz, namely the *II–V–I* (chords built from the 2nd, 5th, and 1st degrees of the key), and then see how other chords can be substituted in place of these primary chords. After that we'll cover the form or structure of your favorite songs (for example: Intro, verse, chorus), and learn how to read and write song charts for use in rehearsal or performance situations.

Section 4: Advanced Stuff gets into larger (eleventh and thirteenth) chords and their alterations, as well as more advanced scales (whole-tone and octatonic). We'll also learn how chords from different keys can be used in the same piece of music (with pop, jazz, and classical examples). Then we'll see why upper-structure chord voicings are a staple across a range of contemporary styles, and explore *polychord* (chord-over-chord) arrangements applied to sophisticated jazz examples.

Section 5: Songs contains full piano, guitar, bass, or drum parts for five well-known songs in different styles (which are all included on the CD). Each of these songs demonstrate previously covered theory concepts. See up close how the professionals use their music theory knowledge to create all those cool melodies, chords, and rhythms!

ABOUT THE CD

On the accompanying CD, you'll find recordings of most of the exercises and songs in this book. The single-staff musical examples are recorded with piano or guitar. The grand-staff examples are recorded with piano and feature the left-hand part on the left channel, and the right-hand part on the right channel. (To hear one staff only, just turn down the left or right channel.)

The CD tracks for Section 5 spotlight well-known instrumental parts (piano, guitar, bass, or drums) on some famous songs. On these CD tracks you can hear how each part fits into the overall arrangement of the song!

ICON LEGEND

Included in every *All About* book are several icons to help you on your way. Keep an eye out for these:

AUDIO

This icon signals you to a track on the accompanying CD.

NUTS & BOLTS

This icon highlights important explanations of fundamental concepts.

DON'T FORGET

There's a lot of information in this book and it may be difficult to remember it all. These refreshers will help you stay on track.

TRY THIS

Included with this icon are various suggestions for ways to expand your musical horizons.

DANGER!

Here, you'll learn about some of the pitfalls to avoid, in order to make your learning experience as enjoyable and useful as possible.

EXTRAS

This includes additional information on topics that may be interesting and fruitful, but not necessarily essential.

ORIGINS

Interesting historical blurbs present fun background information.

Basic Theory 101

CHAPTER 1
PITCHES AND THE STAFF

What's Ahead:
- Finding notes on the piano and guitar
- Reading and writing notes on paper
- The treble, bass, and grand staffs

FINDING NOTES ON THE PIANO

We'll start out by learning the note names and where the notes are located on the piano. If you look at the keys on a piano, you'll notice that some are white and some are black, and that they are arranged in an interesting pattern (see right):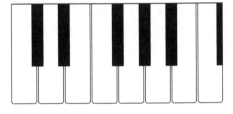

You'll also notice that the black keys are grouped together in sets of two and three, repeatedly up and down the keyboard. This is very handy (not to say essential!), as it enables us to identify the notes and where we are on the keyboard. Or, to put it another way: If the keys just alternated white-black-white-black all the way up and down the keyboard, piano players would be hopelessly lost (and they would probably all have to learn guitar instead)!

It is not essential for you to be a piano player in order to understand music theory. However, beginners are often more comfortable relating theory concepts to the piano, due to the way the notes are laid out on the keyboard. Don't feel left out if you're a guitar player; shortly we'll see how the notes are laid out on the guitar fretboard!

Next we're going to be introduced to the *musical alphabet*. This refers to the letters A, B, C, D, E, F, and G that we use to label the notes (which on the piano are also the names of the white keys). You'll never need to go beyond the letter G, as we "wrap around" again to the letter A. So if someone asks you to find an "H" on the piano (or on any other instrument), you can safely assume that he or she is in desperate need of this book! Now we'll look at the keyboard diagram again, this time with the letters of the musical alphabet added (see bottom right):

You'll notice that this diagram starts and ends on the note C. It just so happens that the white keys on the keyboard collectively make up a C major scale—much more about this later on! As we said before, notice that after we use the letter name G, we return to the beginning of the musical alphabet again to use the letter A. This series of seven letters repeats all the way up and down the keyboard.

We can find the name of each white key relative to the black keys (i.e., to the sets of two or three black keys).

- The note C is always to the left of the two black keys.
- The note D is always in the middle of the two black keys.
- The note E is always to the right of the two black keys.
- The note F is always to the left of the three black keys.
- The note G is always between the first and second key, within the group of three black keys.
- The note A is always between the second and third key, within the group of three black keys.
- The note B is always to the right of the three black keys.

If you have a piano or keyboard handy, you can play a fun exercise to help you identify where these white keys are. Start with any letter of the musical alphabet—let's say, F—then find and play the lowest (leftmost) F on your keyboard. Then play each F successively moving up the keyboard, ending with the highest F. Next, repeat this exercise with each of the other letter names (jump around the musical alphabet, too) until you've covered all the notes.

There's a particularly important "C note" (not a $100 bill!) on the keyboard, called middle C, which as you might expect is in the middle of the piano keyboard. This is a central reference point in our study of music theory, as we will see later on.

Next we'll look at the note names for the black keys on the keyboard. These will use the same letter names (A up to G), but with either a sharp or flat sign added.

The term *sharp* (♯) means to raise the pitch of a note, and the term *flat* (♭) means to lower the pitch. When we move to the right on the keyboard, the notes become progressively higher in pitch, and when we move to the left on the keyboard, the notes become progressively lower.

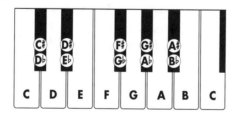

Note that each black key has been given two names: For example, the black key in between C and D can be called either C♯ ("C sharp") or D♭ ("D flat"). In other words, we can sharp (or raise) the pitch C to get to C♯, or we can flat (or lower) the pitch D to get to D♭.

The term *enharmonic* is used to describe the same pitch having more than one name. For example, the note names C♯ and D♭ are enharmonic equivalents. (You can impress your friends at parties by talking about enharmonics!) You might be thinking: "Why would we need to have more than one name for the same note? Wouldn't one name be enough?" Well, believe it or not, depending on which key or scale we are using (much more about keys and scales later on), we may prefer to use one name or the other. Stay tuned!

Now we'll introduce our first interval, the *half step*. If we move from any note on the keyboard to the nearest note on the right or left, this movement will be an interval of a half step. For example, if we start on the note C, the next highest note (i.e., the nearest note to the right) is the black key between C and D (i.e., the note C♯ or D♭); this black key is, therefore, a half step higher than the note C.

When we sharp a note (by adding the "♯" suffix to the note name), we are raising the pitch by a half step; when we flat a note (by adding the "♭" suffix to the note name), we are lowering the pitch by a half step.

Ready for another interval? The next one we'll learn about is called the *octave*. This is the distance between any note and the next note of the same name, either to the right (higher) or to the left (lower). Our diagram, for example, begins and ends on the note C, so the interval between the C on the left and the C on the right is an octave. On a grand piano (or an electronic keyboard of equivalent size) you have a little over seven octaves to play with. On a guitar you have a range of around three-and-a-half octaves, and on a standard four-string bass you have a range of nearly three octaves.

If you count starting from the C on the left of the keyboard to the C on the right, you'll see that there are twelve half steps in one octave. This is a fundamental relationship upon which almost all Western music is based!

You'll notice that certain pairs of white keys on the keyboard don't have a black key in between them (a consequence of the black keys being grouped into sets of two and three). For example, if we start on the note E, the next highest note (i.e., one half step higher) is the note F, because there is no black key between E and F. However, the note F could also be called E♯, as it is the result of raising the pitch E by a half step. So, in fact, alternate note names exist for the notes E, F, B, and C.

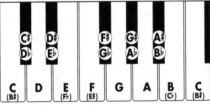

This is another reason why beginning musicians find it easier to relate to the piano when learning note names and enharmonics. For example, the fact that there is no other note between E and F (E up to F is a half step) is visually apparent on the piano keyboard, but not on the guitar fretboard (with all due respect to my many guitarist friends and colleagues).

FINDING NOTES ON THE GUITAR

Speaking of the fretboard, let's now take a look at how the notes are laid out on the guitar. One important difference (among many!), between the layouts of the keyboard and fretboard, is that while any given note only has one location on a piano keyboard, it can have multiple locations on a guitar fretboard. For example, there is only one way to play middle C on the piano, and that is of course to depress the middle C key on the keyboard. By contrast, there are four different places (i.e., combinations of string and fret position) on the guitar where middle C can be played, as we'll see shortly.

But let's start by looking at the notes created by the *open strings* on the guitar (i.e., the natural sound of each string vibrating without any frets being depressed).

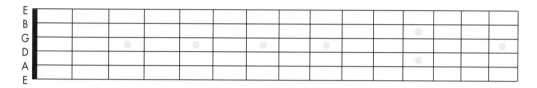

This diagram shows the first fifteen frets of the guitar fretboard. Each fret position is a half step higher than the previous position (equivalent to moving between immediately adjacent keys on the piano). The gray circles on the diagram represent position markers. Notice there are two circles or markers at the twelfth fret. We remember from looking at the keyboard layout that there were twelve half steps in one octave. So, for example, playing the low-E string while fretting the twelfth fret would result in the note E an octave above. Other position markers are typically placed at the third, fifth, seventh, and ninth frets, and the equivalent frets up in the next octave.

The string producing the lowest pitch (E, nearly two octaves below middle C) is shown at the bottom of the diagram, and the other open strings (in ascending order, from the bottom up) produce the pitches A, D, G, B, and E. The high-E string sounds two octaves higher than the low-E string.

Not to forget the bass players out there, the above diagram applies to your instrument, too! The standard four-string bass is tuned to E, A, D, and G (like the bottom four strings of the guitar). However, the strings on the bass sound one octave lower than the strings on the guitar. So if the low-E string on the guitar is nearly two octaves below middle C, then the low-E string on the bass is nearly three octaves below middle C (this is the lowest E on an 88-note keyboard).

We've mentioned already that middle C (**MC**) is located at several positions on the guitar fretboard. Let's go ahead and add to the fretboard diagram all the places you can play this note.

So to play middle C on the guitar, you have some options:

- Depress the A string (second from bottom) at the fifteenth fret.
- Depress the D string (third from bottom) at the tenth fret.
- Depress the G string (third from top) at the fifth fret.
- Depress the B string (second from top) at the second fret.

If you have a guitar handy, pick it up and try these four playing positions. You'll hear that the pitch of the note (middle C) is the same in each case, but the tone color is different. Cool, huh?!

You may remember that (back in Keyboardland) we were shown that the musical alphabet, namely the letters A, B, C, D, E, F, and G are used to name the notes. Well now it's time to add the letters of the musical alphabet to the fretboard diagram.

You can see there is a lot of duplication of notes among the strings of the guitar. For example, fretting the low-E string at the fifth fret gives us the note A, which is the same pitch as the next open string. All of the pitches from the fifth fret upward on the low-E string will, therefore, correspond to pitches available on the A string. Similar relationships occur between other pairs of adjacent strings on the guitar.

So now that we have all of the notes that are equivalent to the white keys on the piano, we'll add the notes in between (which are equivalent to the black keys).

A friendly note to all the guitar players out there: If you're serious about your instrument, you really *do* need to learn where the notes are located on your fretboard. In this book we'll be working with regular music notation, and we'll also see examples of *tablature* (a guitar and bass notation method showing the strings and frets to be used). Although working with tablature can be fun and useful when learning, it's not a substitute for knowing the notes on your instrument and being able to relate them to real music notation. Hopefully if you're already working through this book, then I'm preaching to the choir!

THE STAFF

Now we'll begin to unlock the mysteries of music notation. The good news is that this is actually easier than you think. Once you learn and understand the rules, it all starts to make sense. Music notation will tell you which notes to play, and when and for how long to play them (among other things). We'll start out with the *staff*, which is a collection of five parallel lines.

When notes are written on the staff, they can be written on the lines ("line notes") or on the spaces between the lines ("space notes"). Now we need some way to relate the musical alphabet to the lines and spaces on the staff, so that we know which note corresponds to each line or space. This is achieved by using a *clef*, which is a symbol placed at the beginning of the staff.

THE TREBLE CLEF

The first clef we'll be looking at is the *treble clef*. This clef is used to notate music for piano and guitar (as well as other instruments). For piano music, the treble clef is used to represent the notes in the upper portion of the piano keyboard (from around middle C upward).

This clef is a G clef. If you take a close look at the clef symbol, you'll notice the lower part of the symbol circles around the second line from the bottom of the staff. This clef is telling you that the second staff line from the bottom represents the G above middle C. Once we know that, we can then work out which letter names are allocated to the other lines and spaces on the staff.

Note that the G above middle C is shown as the second "line note" in the left-hand diagram. So, the other letter names are allocated to the remaining lines and spaces on the staff, according to the musical alphabet. For example, the next note above G on the keyboard is A (as we "wrap around" to the start of the alphabet) and, if you look in the right-hand diagram, A is the second note shown; it is the next note moving up the staff from G.

extras

It's possible to use mnemonic sayings to get acquainted with the notes in the treble clef. For example, the "line notes" in the treble clef (**E**–**G**–**B**–**D**–**F**) could correspond to the phrase "**E**very **G**ood **B**oy **D**oes **F**ine." Also, the "space notes" (**F**–**A**–**C**–**E**) spell the word "FACE." While these mnemonics may be fun and handy at the very initial stages of learning, they are not suitable as a long-term way to learn the notes if you're serious about music. It's much better to develop a relative or positional technique to learn the notes on the staff, combined with drills using flashcards… more about this shortly.

So far we've only been dealing with the notes on the staff corresponding to the white keys on the piano keyboard. Next we'll see how to notate the black keys. Earlier in this chapter we named the black keys with either a sharp (♯) or a flat (♭). For example, the black key between F and G could be called either F♯ or G♭. Now we'll see how these notes are notated on the staff.

The first note shown above is F, and the next note is F♯. Notice that F♯ is still in the F space, but now with a sharp sign (♯) to its left. Similarly, following the G we have a G♭, which is still on the G line, but now with a flat sign (♭) to its left.

THE BASS CLEF

On to our next clef, the *bass clef*. This clef is used to notate music for piano and bass (as well as other instruments). For piano music, the bass clef is used to represent the notes in the lower portion of the piano keyboard (from around middle C downward).

This clef is an F clef. If you take a close look at the clef symbol, you'll notice that the clef seems to be attached to the second line from the top of the staff. This clef is telling you that the second staff line from the top represents the F below middle C. Once we know that, we can then work out which letter names are allocated to the other lines and spaces on the staff.

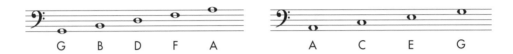

G B D F A   A C E G

Note that the fourth "line note" in the left-hand diagram is F, as this is on the second line from the top of the staff (between the two dots in the clef symbol). Again, the other letter names are allocated to the remaining lines and spaces on the staff according to the musical alphabet.

extras

It's possible to use mnemonics to get acquainted with the notes in the bass clef, too. For example, the "line notes" in the bass clef (**G**–**B**–**D**–**F**–**A**) could correspond to the phrase "**G**ood **B**oys **D**o **F**ine **A**lways," and the "space notes" in the bass clef (**A**–**C**–**E**–**G**) could correspond to the phrase "**A**ll **C**ows **E**at **G**rass."

THE GRAND STAFF

Fasten your seat belts... now it's time to join the treble and bass clefs together to create what is known as the *grand staff*. This is normally how piano music is written, with the right hand playing the treble-clef part and the left hand playing the bass-clef part. Notice there is a line connecting the two staffs together; a bracket is also added, signifying that the staffs are grouped together.

extras

Even if you are not a piano player, I recommend becoming familiar with the notes in both treble and bass clefs. It's always nice, when I'm rehearsing or performing, if the bass player can read treble clef and the guitarist can read bass clef. It comes in handy sometimes, and it indicates an extra level of professionalism!

MIDDLE C AND LEDGER LINES

Now we'll return to the note middle C. It turns out that this note is just a little below the treble clef, and just a little above the bass clef. So we need to extend the clefs by adding another small staff line (known as a *ledger line*) to accommodate this note.

It's important to understand that *both* of the notes shown to the right are middle C. We know that the bottom "line note" in the treble clef is E. Well, if we go down one letter name to D, this note would sit right below the bottom staff line; then one further note down to C would need an extra staff line below—which is exactly what the ledger line is. Similarly, we know that the top "line note" in the bass clef is A. If we go up one letter name to B, this note would sit right above the top staff line, and one further note up to C would need the ledger line.

Middle C is both the first ledger line below the treble clef and the first ledger line above the bass clef. This important relationship will help you get oriented to the grand staff.

LEARNING THE NOTE NAMES

Now we'll develop some techniques to learn the note names across the range of the grand staff. In my classes and books I often talk about developing "guideposts" to help you recognize the notes. Our first set of guideposts consists of all the C notes (no, these are still not $100 bills!) within a four-octave range, centered around middle C.

Comparing this to the previous diagram, we notice that the middle Cs are still there, but we now have some extra notes. We remember that the second space from the top of the treble clef is C (an octave above middle C), and that the second space from the bottom of the bass clef is C (an octave below middle C). The notes at the very top and bottom are also Cs, and require two ledger lines each.

Learning and memorizing where these Cs are on the grand staff is fairly easy—notice that there is a "mirror-image," or symmetrical relationship, on either side of middle C. These guideposts are handy when figuring out other notes on the grand staff—at least you could count up or down within the musical alphabet from the nearest C.

The next stage is to memorize some more guideposts. How about adding all of the Gs within the four-octave range? Let's try it.

Now the stack of notes looks a bit more intense, but all we've done is add two Gs in the treble clef (on the second line from the bottom, and right above the top line) and two Gs in the bass clef (in the top space, and on the bottom line). Although these are not exactly symmetrical on either side of middle C, they're pretty close—and they're easy to visually memorize.

I would recommend that you first learn and memorize where all the Cs are located, then where all the Gs are located. So when you're trying to figure out other notes in either the treble or bass clefs, you'll never be more than two notes away from a C or a G, and you can work up or down the musical alphabet as needed. This is, of course, only a temporary method, until you gradually learn all of the notes individually; however, it's still way better than fooling around with mnemonics for note names—at least in my humble opinion!

Let's now fill in the blanks and take a look at all of the notes between the lowest and highest Cs shown in the previous examples.

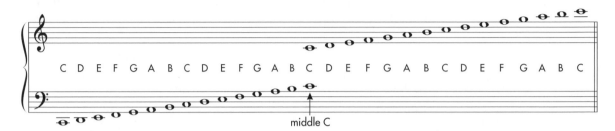

C D E F G A B C D E F G A B C D E F G A B C D E F G A B C

middle C

You should make it a goal to learn all of these notes individually. On the road toward this goal, learning the guideposts in the previous examples will definitely help you.

Another way to increase your note-learning and memorization is by using flashcards that you can buy at your local music store. Each card has a note written in treble or bass clef on the front, and the note name shown on the back. The idea is to name the note as quickly as you can, and then check the back of the card to see if you're right. Simple, but effective.

One last thing to mention in this chapter: When a piano player reads a note on the staff (for instance, the middle C in the center of the previous diagram), that is the exact note that is heard. "So what," I hear you ask, "Why *wouldn't* it be?" Well, believe it or not, there are some instruments that produce a note different from the one being read. These instruments are referred to as *transposing instruments*, because the note being read is *transposed* (or moved) by a particular interval (more about intervals shortly). The guitar and bass are both transposing instruments, in that the notes they sound are one octave lower than the notes they read. So if you were writing a guitar part and you wanted the sound of the D right above middle C, you would actually write the D an octave higher (on the second line from the top of the treble clef). Similarly, if you were writing a bass part and you wanted the sound of the G on the bottom line of the bass clef, you would actually write the G an octave higher (in the top space of the bass clef).

CHAPTER 2
TIME SIGNATURES AND RHYTHMS

What's Ahead:

- Dividing music into measures
- The 4/4 time signature
- Note lengths, rests, and rhythmic counting (whole, half, quarter, eighth, and sixteenth notes)
- Dotted and tied notes

DIVIDING MUSIC INTO MEASURES

In the last chapter we dealt with the pitches of the notes (i.e., how high or low they are), and where they are positioned on the staff. Now we'll learn about the vital part that rhythm plays in music, and in how we notate the music. Most styles of music have a rhythmic *beat* or pulse to them. When you tap your feet along with a piece of music, most likely you are tapping along with the beat. These beats are grouped into *measures* (or *bars*) when the music is notated. Here is an example of a treble staff with *barlines* separating the measures:

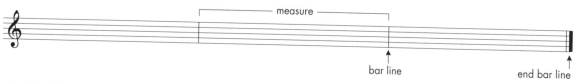

4/4 TIME SIGNATURE

Most of the music that you will play will have four beats to the measure. This means that when we count the beats, after we get to "4" we will go back to "1" (i.e., we will count: "1, 2, 3, 4, 1, 2, 3, 4," etc.). By now you're probably thinking that we need a way to let whoever's reading the music know how many beats there are in each measure. Well, you'd be right: we use a *time signature* placed right after the clef sign.

The top number of the time signature ("4" in this case) indicates how many beats there are in each measure—these are where you would normally tap your foot! The bottom number of the time signature ("4" in this case) indicates which *rhythmic value* is assigned to the beat.

We're about to encounter different *rhythmic values* (note lengths), such as quarter notes, half notes, and whole notes. The "4" at the bottom of the time signature means that each beat in the measure will be a quarter note. The 4/4 time signature, therefore, means that there are four quarter-note beats per measure (more about quarter notes in a minute...).

The 4/4 time signature is also referred to as *common time*, probably because it is overwhelmingly the most common time signature in music. Common time also has its own time signature symbol.

So any time you see this "C" symbol used as a time signature, that's equivalent to 4/4 time—you can use either one and it means the same thing. Later, in Chapter 8, we'll see some more time signatures (other than 4/4).

INTRODUCING NOTE LENGTHS: QUARTER, HALF, AND WHOLE NOTES

Now we need to get into *note lengths* (the number of beats each note lasts). Let's first have a look at the *quarter note*, which lasts for one beat:

The quarter note is written as a black (or "filled-in") notehead, with a long stem attached.

So why is this called a quarter note? Well, we already said that music most often uses the *4/4 time signature* (i.e., has four beats per measure). So in this case, the note lasting for one beat is also a quarter of the measure. Notice the counting shown under the notes ("1, 2, 3, 4"): Each note is held for one beat.

Next we'll look at the *half note*, which lasts for two beats:

The half note is written as a white (or "empty") notehead, with a long stem attached.

Similar logic is behind the naming of the half note: Since it lasts for two beats, it is also half of a 4/4 measure. Again, the count is shown under the notes: Each note is held for two beats.

You probably noticed that both the quarter notes and half notes have stems, in this case to the right of the notehead and going upward. However, once the notehead gets to the middle line of the staff or above, the stem is then placed to the left of the note and goes downward.

Next we'll look at the *whole note*, which lasts for four beats:

The whole note is written as a white (or "empty") notehead, without a stem.

Similar logic is behind the naming of the whole note: It lasts for four beats, or one whole 4/4 measure. The count is shown under the notes: The whole note is held for four beats.

COUNTING RHYTHMS WITH QUARTER, HALF, AND WHOLE NOTES

Next we have an example written in 4/4 time that combines different rhythmic values. We'll see how to count our way through it.

Notice the counting under the staff: We have one number (one beat) under each quarter note, two numbers (two beats) under each half note, and four numbers (four beats) under each whole note.

Listen to **Track 1** on the CD, and clap these rhythms while counting along. Notice that there is one "count-off measure" on the CD, before the music starts: Four clicks to let you know the tempo, and where to come in. If you have an instrument handy, you can play along with the example, too.

> The sum of all the rhythmic values in each measure has to match the time signature (which in this case indicates four beats). For example, in the third measure above, we have two quarter notes (one beat each) and one half note (two beats): 1 + 1 + 2 = 4 beats total, so we're okay.

INTRODUCING RESTS: QUARTER, HALF, AND WHOLE RESTS

Sometimes the music needs to take a break, rather than keep playing notes continuously. This is shown in the music with *rests*, which let you know how many beats to rest (or not to play). Here are some examples:

These rests last for one, two, and four beats, respectively. Now we'll combine some notes and rests together.

Listen to **Track 2** on the CD, and clap the rhythm while counting along. If you're playing this example on your instrument, make sure you play the notes, but don't play during the rests. Again there is one "count-off measure" on the CD, before the music starts.

The sum of all the rhythmic values (now including notes and rests) in each measure still have to match the time signature. For example, in the seventh measure of **Track 2**, we have one half rest (two beats), one quarter note (one beat), and one quarter rest (one beat): 2 + 1 + 1 = 4 beats total, so again we're okay.

EIGHTH NOTES AND RESTS

Next up is the *eighth note*, which lasts for half a beat. The eighth note is written as a black (or "filled-in") notehead, with a long stem attached and either a *flag* (if the note is by itself), or a *beam* (if the note is joined to other notes). Sometimes the beam may join two eighth notes together within one beat, or the beam may join four eighth notes within two successive beats.

The next example shows the various ways eighth notes can be notated. Notice the rhythmic counting underneath the staff, which now uses an "&" between each of the beat numbers ("&" is what we count for notes that fall halfway between the beats).

Listen to **Track 3** on the CD, and play or clap this eighth-note rhythmic pattern while counting along. As usual, you have one "count-off measure" on the CD, before the music starts, and the click is on every quarter-note beat. This means that you will be playing in between the clicks when playing on the "&"s.

In contemporary rhythmic situations where eighth notes are used, the notes falling on the beats (i.e., on "1," "2," "3," or "4") are referred to as *downbeats*, and the notes falling on the "&"s are referred to as *upbeats*. Also, the eighth note following beat 1 is referred to as the "& of 1," the eighth note following beat 2 is referred to as the "& of 2," and so on. Chapter 8 contains much more about upbeats and downbeats.

So why are these guys called eighth notes? We saw earlier that note lengths were named according to what fraction of a 4/4 measure they used. Well, an eighth note (lasting half of one beat) takes up one-eighth of a 4/4 measure. Eighth notes may also be beamed (or joined) to other smaller note values, such as sixteenth notes (more about sixteenths soon).

Now we'll get acquainted with the *eighth rest* (which, as you might expect, also lasts for half a beat).

Next we'll look at another melody, this one including some eighth notes and rests.

Clap or play the above example while counting, then listen to **Track 4**. If you're playing an instrument, make sure that you don't play during the rests.

DOTTED AND TIED NOTES

Now we will go boldly into the realm of *dotted notes*! Whenever a dot is placed after a note, it adds half as much to the note's rhythmic value or length (or, if you're a math whiz, it multiplies the existing length by 1.5). Let's check out the following example:

dotted half
(3 beats)   dotted quarter
(1½ beats)   dotted eighth
(¾ beats)

Without the dot, the first note would just be a half note (lasting for two beats); but with the dot, we add half as much to the original length, so the note now lasts for three beats. Similarly, the dotted quarter note lasts for one-and-a-half beats (instead of just one beat), and the dotted eighth note lasts for three-fourths of a beat (instead of just half a beat).

Next we will see how these dotted half and dotted quarter notes can be used in a melody. (Later we'll see an example with some dotted eighth notes.) If we use a *dotted half note* (three beats) together with a quarter note (one beat), the resulting total of four beats will fill a 4/4 measure. If we use a *dotted quarter note* (one-and-a-half beats) together with an eighth note (half a beat), the resulting total of two beats could occupy the first or second half of a 4/4 measure. These are extremely common rhythmic combinations, as shown in this melody:

1 – 2 – 3   4   1 – 2 & 3 – 4   1 – 2 & 3   4   1   2 – 3 – 4

Clap or play the above example while counting, then listen to **Track 5** to check your work.

Now we're ready to look at *tied notes*. When two notes of the same pitch are joined by a curved line, they are tied together. This means that the second note is not played separately; instead, the note lasts for the combined length of both notes. Check out the following example:

1   2   3   4   &   1   2   3   –   4

Listen to **Track 6** and clap or play the eighth-note rhythm pattern while counting along. Note that the C, on the "& of 4" in the first measure, lasts right up until the start of beat 2 in the second measure. In other words, this tied note lasts for one-and-a-half beats.

This example shows the most common situation in which a tie is needed: When the note is longer than the remaining number of beats in the measure. In this case, the last C in the first measure falls on the "& of 4" (so there is only half a beat left in the measure), and yet we need the note to last for one-and-a-half beats. So tying across the barline to the quarter note in the next measure neatly solves this problem.

Now we'll look at another example involving tied notes:

Try playing or clapping the above example, and then listen to Track 7 to see if you got it right.

"But wait!" I hear you cry. "Why did we need that first tie? Couldn't we have used just a dotted quarter note (which lasts for one-and-a-half beats) starting on the "& of 2" in the first measure? There's no barline anywhere in sight!" Whoa... calm down a minute! The reason we did it this way is to show the start of beat 3. That is to say, whether or not we are actually playing on beat 3, it is very good practice and courtesy to show a note or rest right on beat 3. This greatly aids sightreading, as players can scan quickly through the music and pick out beats 1 and 3 (sometimes called the *primary beats*) in 4/4 time. If you're ever preparing charts for other musicians (maybe to demo or perform your own songs), they will definitely appreciate it if you do this.

SIXTEENTH NOTES AND RESTS

The *sixteenth note* lasts for a quarter of a beat, and is written as a black (or "filled-in") notehead, with a long stem attached, and either a double flag (if the note is by itself), or a double beam (if the note is joined to other notes). Sometimes the beams may join a pair of sixteenth notes together, or the beams may join all the sixteenth notes within one beat.

Now that we're dividing the beat into four pieces, we need a different counting method. So the rhythmic counting now uses the three symbols "e," "&," and "a" between each of the numbered beats.

Listen to **Track 8** and clap or play this sixteenth-note rhythm while counting aloud. Now there are four notes for every metronome click. Try to space the notes as evenly as possible between the downbeats.

A little while ago we talked about combining dotted notes with other notes (i.e., dotted half + quarter = four beats; dotted quarter + eighth = two beats). Well, now that we have the sixteenth note, we can combine it with a dotted eighth note (lasting for three-fourths of a beat) for a total duration of one beat. The next melody includes some of these dotted-eighth/sixteenth-note combinations.

Listen to **Track 9** and clap or play this sixteenth-note rhythm while counting aloud.

It's good practice to count all of the sixteenth notes (i.e., "1 e & a, 2 e & a," etc.) in the **Track 9** example as you clap or play it, even though you are not using all of these rhythmic subdivisions. That way, when a sixteenth note comes along (for instance, the D in the first measure), you'll be ready for it!

Next we'll get acquainted with the *sixteenth rest* (which, as you have probably guessed, lasts for a quarter of a beat). This rest looks like the eighth rest, except that it has two flags instead of one.

To conclude this chapter we'll look at a melody that combines quarter notes and rests, eighth notes and rests, and sixteenth notes and rests. Note the counting under the staff, and the new sixteenth rests (each lasting for a quarter of a beat) in both measures.

Listen to **Track 10** and clap or play the example while counting along. As before, make sure that you don't play during the rests. And don't forget to have fun!

CHAPTER 3

CHAPTER 3
MAJOR SCALES, KEYS, AND KEY SIGNATURES

> **What's Ahead:**
> - Building major scales
> - Finding major scales on the piano and guitar
> - Major key signatures and accidentals
> - The circle of 5ths/4ths (or circle of keys)

THE BUILDING BLOCKS OF SCALES

In this chapter we're going to learn about the *major scale*, which is the most commonly used scale in Western music. Most famous melodies that you know are constructed from major scales.

A *scale* is a sequence of notes created using a specific set of intervals. Most scales (including the major scale) are built using half and whole steps, although some scales contain larger intervals. Back in Chapter 1 we saw that the half step was the interval between any note and the nearest note either above or below. Now we will define the whole step as double the size of a half step.

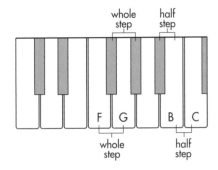

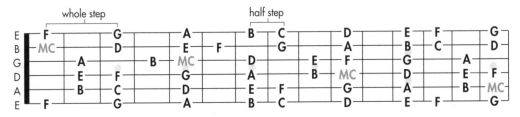

Notice that each whole step is equivalent to two half steps. For example, the whole step F–G includes two half steps (F–F♯ and F♯–G). So now that we have our half and whole steps figured out, we can build all of our major scales pretty easily!

BUILDING MAJOR SCALES

We are now going to build a C major scale, using a specific sequence of whole and half steps (W = whole step; H = half step).

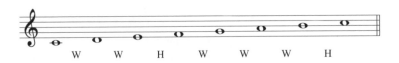

nuts
& bolts

The major scale is a seven-note scale (i.e., there are seven different pitches). Notice that we have used each of the letter names in the musical alphabet once.

The major scale should be a familiar and recognizable sound. Your inner ear already understands the sound of this scale (assuming you've had some exposure to mainstream music). Now we'll start this pattern of whole and half steps from F, to create the F major scale:

Track 11
(0:07)

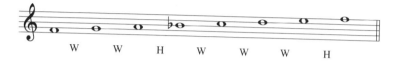

Notice that we now have the note B♭ as the 4th degree of this scale. This is because we need a half step between the 3rd and 4th degrees. We already have A as the 3rd degree, and we need to use the next letter name (B) for the next note, so we flat the B (to B♭) to get the required half step above A.

Next we'll use the same method to build a G major scale.

Track 11
(0:14)

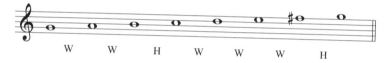

Notice that we now have the note F♯ as the 7th degree of this scale. This is because we need a whole step between the 6th and 7th degrees. We already have E as the 6th degree, and we need to use the next letter name (F) for the next note, so we sharp the F (to F♯) to get the required whole step above E.

Here are all of the major scales, for your reference:

Track 11
(0:21)

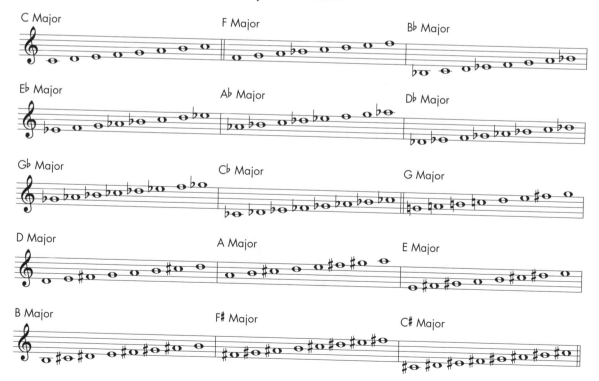

As we said, many well-known tunes are built from major scales. Here's an excerpt from Offenbach's familiar "Can Can Polka," which uses a complete descending C major scale.

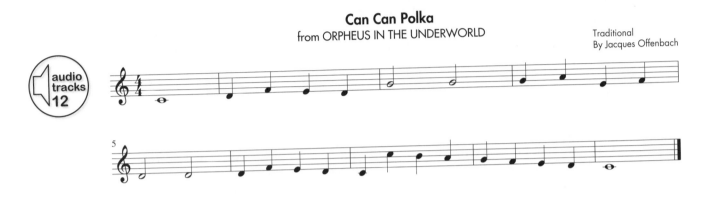

Can Can Polka
from ORPHEUS IN THE UNDERWORLD

Traditional
By Jacques Offenbach

FINDING MAJOR SCALES ON THE PIANO AND GUITAR

Now we'll revisit the C, F, and G major scales to see where they are located on the keyboard and fretboard.

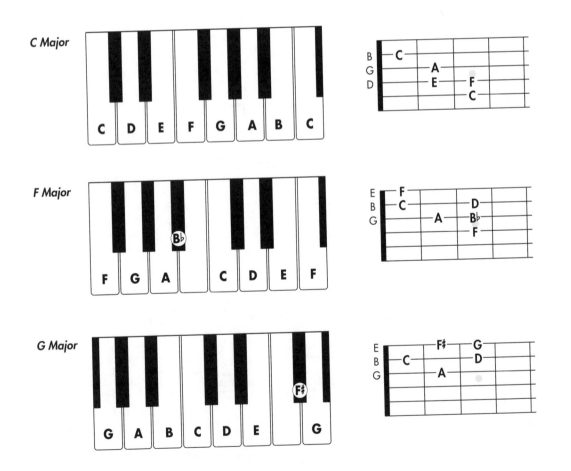

Note that when we build the C major scale on the piano, it so happens that we use all of the white keys on the keyboard. But when we build the major-scale interval pattern (using whole and half steps) from any note other than C, we get a mixture of black and white keys (for example, the F and G major scales each contain one black key).

Bear in mind that the same note can be played in different places on the guitar fretboard (as we saw in Chapter 1), so the major-scale patterns shown for guitar give only one of the numerous ways in which each scale can be played.

LABELING THE MAJOR SCALE DEGREES

Different conventions are in use for naming the *degrees* within the major scale. We can use:

- numbers (i.e., 1, 2, 3, etc.);
- solfege syllables (i.e., DO, RE, MI, etc.);
- traditional classical names (i.e., tonic, supertonic, mediant, etc.).

Here are all three labeling styles shown with respect to the C major scale:

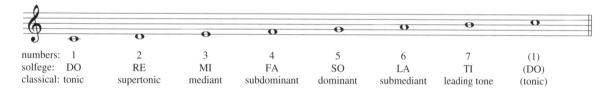

numbers:	1	2	3	4	5	6	7	(1)
solfege:	DO	RE	MI	FA	SO	LA	TI	(DO)
classical:	tonic	supertonic	mediant	subdominant	dominant	submediant	leading tone	(tonic)

Of these methods, the numbers are probably used the most, and the solfege syllables are also useful when doing vocal drills and ear training. (We'll have more to say about solfege and scale degrees later!)

MAJOR KEY SIGNATURES

When we play the C major scale, we can hear that the note C sounds like the "home base" (or *tonic*) of the scale. If a song uses the C major scale, it is most likely to be in the key of C.

A *key signature* is a group of sharps or flats at the beginning of the music that lets you know which key you are in (and which major scale to use). You may not have noticed the key signature used in the "Can Can Polka." That's because it uses the C major scale, and is therefore in the key of C (the key signature for C major has no sharps or flats). Let's compare this to the key signature for F major (see bottom left).

C major

Relating this to the F major scale we built earlier, we remember that we needed B♭ as the 4th degree of the scale. So the key signature reminds you to play B♭ (instead of B) when playing in the key of F. That way we don't need to keep writing flat signs for all the B♭s that come up in the music. Pretty cool labor-saving device, huh?

F major

Now we'll look at the key signature for G major (see right).

Relating this to the G major scale we built earlier, we remember that we needed F♯ as the 7th degree of the scale. So the key signature reminds you to play F♯ (instead of F) when playing in the key of G. That way we don't need to keep writing sharp signs for all the F♯s that come up in the music.

G major

Here are all of the major key signatures, for your reference:

You'll notice that each key signature consists of either flats or sharps, but not both mixed together. This is because there is no major scale that needs both flats and sharps.

Now if you're reading a piece of music and you see a key signature at the beginning, it's very handy (not to say essential!) for you to recognize the key that you're in. That way you'll know what major scale to use, and which flats or sharps you'll need to play.

In flat key signatures, the second to last flat in the key signature is the key that you're in. For example, looking at the key signature of A♭ major, we see there are four flats. The second to last flat in the key signature is A♭, your key! For sharp keys, the last sharp in the key signature is the 7th degree of the key that you're in, so you just need to go up a half step from this note (using the next letter name in the musical alphabet) to find the key. For example, looking at the key signature of A major, we see there are three sharps. The last sharp in the key signature is G♯, so if we go up a half step from this note (and go to the next letter name) we get to A, our key!

ACCIDENTALS

Key signatures are a convenient way of indicating a major scale used in a piece of music. But what happens when we want to move outside of that scale? Then we need to use *accidentals*. These are sharp, flat, or natural signs placed in the music that will contradict the key signature at that point. The *natural* sign contradicts a sharp or a flat that would otherwise be required by the key signature—so the term "B natural" (B♮) just means plain old B (yes, the white key, if you're sitting at the piano)!

An accidental will be in use for the remainder of the measure in which it is introduced, and will then be cancelled by the next barline (or beforehand if necessary, by a sharp, flat, or natural that re-establishes the key signature). Let's now look at an example in the key of F that uses accidentals:

(1) This is the note B♭, as required by the key signature.

(2) This is the note B♮, which contradicts the key signature.

(3) This is the note B♭, as required by the key signature. The barline cancelled the previous accidental (a courtesy accidental is placed as a reminder).

(4) This is the note B♮, which contradicts the key signature.

(5) This is still the note B♮. The accidental is still in force until the next barline.

(6) This is the note B♭, which needed a flat sign to cancel out the accidental, as we're still in the same measure.

So watch out for those accidentals! But if you follow these rules, you should do just fine.

THE CIRCLE OF 5THS/4THS (OR CIRCLE OF KEYS)

The major key signatures can be derived by using the *circle of 5ths* (which is also called the *circle of 4ths* or *circle of keys*). You should be aware that there are different interpretations of what is meant by this circle (across a wide range of textbooks and methods), so I will try to cover these interpretations in a way that will make sense! First of all, let's start with a basic circle diagram.

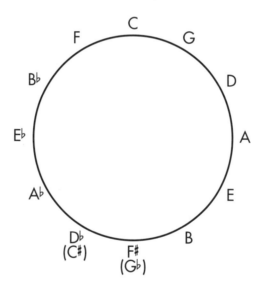

Each of the entries around the circle can represent either individual notes or major keys. Notice in this diagram that the sharp keys (G, D, A, etc.) are written to the right of the C at the top, and the flat keys (F, B♭, E♭, etc.) are written to the left. This is how the circle appears in the majority of textbooks. However, some modern methods (including theory texts by *Dick Grove*, a leading American music educator of the late 20th century) show the circle written the other way (i.e., with sharp keys to the left, and flat keys to the right). I don't think it actually matters which way you write it, as long as you understand the concepts and relationships I am about to present!

The simplest and most traditional interpretation of the circle of 5ths is as a series of ascending perfect 5ths between individual notes, moving clockwise (starting from the C at the top). Don't worry if you're not yet sure what a perfect 5th is—all intervals will be covered in detail shortly. For now, just be aware that C up to G is a *perfect 5th* (G is the 5th degree of a C major scale), G up to D is another perfect 5th, and so on. If you continue this pattern all around the circle, you will eventually get back to the starting point, C.

It starts to get a bit more interesting if we assign a major scale (or key) to each stage of the circle. It turns out that neighboring scales on the circle share most of their notes. Or, to put it another way, only one note is different between immediate neighbors on the circle. For example, earlier in this chapter we built the C major scale, which had no sharps or flats. The F major scale (to the left of C major on the circle) had one flat, and therefore only one note different from the C major scale. Similarly, the G major scale (to the right of C major on the circle) had one sharp, and again only one note different from the C major scale. Most tunes that change keys do so by moving to a key that is adjacent on the circle, so that the original major scale is not completely altered. That way the listener has more chance of keeping up with what's happening!

Once major keys are assigned to each stage of the circle, we can use the circle to help us remember the key signatures we covered earlier.

As we count around the circle, moving clockwise from C, each successive sharp key has an extra sharp in the key signature. For example, the key of G has one sharp, the key of D has two sharps, and so on. This sequence ends with the key of C♯, which has seven sharps. Similarly, moving counterclockwise from C, each successive flat key has an extra flat in the key signature. For example, the key of F has one flat, the key of B♭ has two flats, and so on. This sequence ends with the key of C♭, which has seven flats.

Note the overlap zone at the bottom of the circle, where alternate (enharmonic) keys exist (i.e., D♭/C♯, F♯/G♭, and B/C♭).

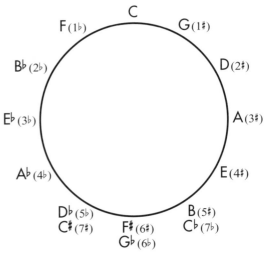

We can also use the circle to figure out which sharps or flats occur in a key signature, and in which specific order.

For the sharp keys, we cumulatively take the 7th degree of each major scale, moving clockwise around the circle from the top. For example, to figure out the key signature for E major (which has four sharps), we would take the 7th degree of G (F♯), the 7th degree of D (C♯), the 7th degree of A (G♯), and finally the 7th degree of E (D♯). This gives us the four sharps in the order needed: F♯, C♯, G♯, and D♯.

For the flat keys, we cumulatively take the 4th degree of each major scale, moving counterclockwise around the circle from the top. For example, to figure out the key signature for E♭ major (which has three flats), we would take the 4th degree of F (B♭), the 4th degree of B♭ (E♭), and finally the 4th degree of E♭ (A♭). This gives us the three flats in the order needed: B♭, E♭, and A♭.

To conclude, we'll look at a more sophisticated interpretation of the circle, one often used by contemporary musicians and educators. We've already seen that each stage of the circle can represent a major key. So rather than thinking of the circle as simply a series of intervals, we can instead think of it as a series of keys. For example, we could move from the key of C to the key of G (moving clockwise on the circle), then to the key of D, and so on. One of the simplest and most common ways to do this in contemporary styles is to build major triads from each stage of the circle (much more about triads shortly). Each time we land at a new stage on the circle, it typically feels like we've arrived at a new key's tonic. It is useful, therefore, to consider the relationship between the previous stage of the circle and the current stage at which we have arrived. This is where a more contemporary (and, I believe, more useful) definition of the circle of 5ths and circle of 4ths comes into play.

For instance, the Jimi Hendrix song "Hey Joe" repeats the same major-triad progression throughout the song: C–G–D–A–E (moving clockwise around the circle). When we move from C to G, it feels like we're in the key of G, so we can define the C–G movement as a IV–I relationship in G. Then the next G–D movement is a IV–I in D, and so on. The term *circle of 4ths* is used to reference this type of harmonic movement between chords and keys (i.e., circle of 4ths = IV–I relationship).

Well, not exactly danger... but be careful to avoid confusion here! The traditional definition of circle of 5ths (used by entry-level and college texts) refers to the interval movement C–G–D–etc., as outlined at the beginning of this section. Now we're saying that the movement between chords/keys of C–G–D–etc. is actually a circle of 4ths, due to the implied IV–I relationships. Some instructors make this distinction by referring to the melodic and harmonic circles, respectively. It's really only terminology at the end of the day—just be aware of the different interpretations that are out there!

Continuing with the harmonic aspect of the circle, if we move between the chords G–C–F (as in the Toto song "Rosanna"), this counterclockwise movement is a series of V–I relationships, eventually leading us to the key of F. The term *circle of 5ths* is used to reference this type of harmonic movement between chords and keys (i.e., circle of 5ths = V–I relationship).

Many songs use these chordal movements around the circle, especially the circle of 4ths. Some notable examples are:

Rolling Stones, "Jumpin' Jack Flash"   C–G–D–A (circle of 4ths)
Simple Minds, "Don't You Forget About Me"   D♭–A♭–E♭–B♭ (circle of 4ths)
Talking Heads, "And She Was"   E–A–D–A–E (circle of 5ths and circle of 4ths)

CHAPTER 4
INTERVALS AND MELODIES

What's Ahead:
- Creating and altering intervals
- Intervals in melodies
- Melody characteristics

INTRODUCTION TO INTERVALS

An *interval* is the distance between any two notes. We've already gotten to know a few intervals in the earlier chapters, such as the half and whole steps. Now we're going to derive some larger intervals, based on the visual distance between the notes on the staff. Let's look at the interval on the right, and figure out what it is.

The first thing we need to determine is the interval number. To do this, we count up from the bottom note (starting at 1), and count each successive line or space until we get to the top note.

- The first note shown is C: this is 1.
- The next note up (immediately below the bottom line of the staff) would be D: this is 2.
- The next note up (on the bottom line of the staff) would be E: this is 3.
- The next note up (in the bottom space of the staff) would be F: this is 4.
- The next note up (on the second line from the bottom of the staff) would be G: this is 5.
- The next note up (in the second space from the bottom of the staff) is A: this is 6.

The last number was 6; therefore the interval from C up to A is a 6th. Now, there are different types of 6ths (the most common being major and minor), but more about this in a moment!

Here's another interval—actually two intervals, both of which are C up to E:

Again, to determine the interval number, we start at 1 and count upward, including all the lines and spaces. So on the left we have a 3rd, and on the right we have a 10th. Both of these intervals consist of C up to E, but the E on the right is one octave higher than the E on the left. Therefore, a 3rd plus an octave is equal to a 10th.

The difference between these two interval numbers ("3" and "10") is seven, which leads to the following rule: Adding (or subtracting) seven to an interval number increases (or decreases) the size of the interval by one octave.

INTERVALS IN THE MAJOR SCALE

You remember the C major scale that we built in the last chapter? Now we'll look at the interval between the starting note (C) and each of the other notes in this scale.

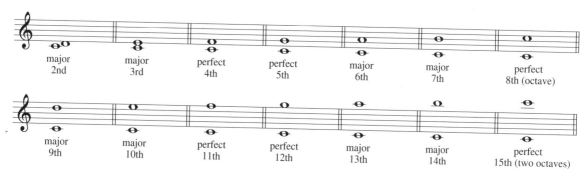

major 2nd | major 3rd | perfect 4th | perfect 5th | major 6th | major 7th | perfect 8th (octave)

major 9th | major 10th | perfect 11th | perfect 12th | major 13th | major 14th | perfect 15th (two octaves)

Notice that the interval numbers (2nd, 3rd, 4th, etc.) are shown below each interval, together with an interval description, which is either *major* or *perfect*. The 4th, 5th, and octave (and 11th, 12th, and two octaves) are the perfect intervals, and the remaining intervals are major.

The perfect intervals have this name because they occur prominently in nature's *overtone series* (the upper harmonics that result from natural acoustic vibrations). The name "major" is given to the other intervals occurring in the major scale.

ALTERED INTERVALS

When we alter the intervals that occur within the major scale, we get minor, augmented, and diminished intervals. To understand these intervals, we first need to learn about *double flats* and *double sharps*.

B ----------- B flat ------- B double flat

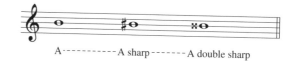

A ----------- A sharp ------ A double sharp

We already saw in Chapter 1 that if we flat the note B by a half step, we get B♭. Now if we flat by a further half step, we get B♭♭ ("B double flat"), which is in fact equivalent to the note A. "So," I hear you ask, "Why can't we just use A then?" Well, believe it or not, there are some key and scale contexts in which it is better to use the double accidental: For example, if we are flatting a note that already appears as a flat in the key signature. Similarly, if we sharp A by a half step, we get A♯, and if we then sharp by a further half step we get A✕ ("A double sharp"), which, is equivalent to B. Note that the *double flat* symbol is two flats signs together, but the *double sharp* symbol is not two sharp signs!

Now I'm going to give you the five rules for figuring out altered intervals.

Rule 1: A major interval reduced by half step becomes a minor interval.

major 7th | minor 7th

We've already seen that C up to B is a major 7th. When we reduce this by a half step, we get a minor 7th.

Rule 2: A minor interval reduced by a further half step becomes a diminished interval.

Track 14
(0:07)

In the previous example we saw that C up to B♭ is a minor 7th. When we reduce this by a further half step, we get a diminished 7th.

This interval is still called a 7th because the letter names written on the staff are C up to B. However, we have already seen that the B♭♭ is equivalent to A, and that C up to A would be a major 6th. We can say, therefore, that the major 6th and diminished 7th are equivalent to one another. These intervals sound the same, but are written differently.

Speaking of the major 6th, let's use it in the next example.

Rule 3: A major interval increased by a half step becomes an augmented interval.

Track 14
(0:14)

Previously we saw that C up to A is a major 6th. When we increase this by a half step, we get an augmented 6th.

So far we've been altering major and minor intervals. Now it's time to alter some perfect intervals.

Rule 4: A perfect interval reduced by a half step becomes a diminished interval.

Track 14
(0:21)

Earlier we saw that C up to G is a perfect 5th. When we reduce this by a half step, we get a diminished 5th.

Rule 5: A perfect interval increased by a half step becomes an augmented interval.

Track 14
(0:28)

We saw before that C up to F is a perfect 4th. When we increase this by a half step, we get an augmented 4th.

Notice there are some more intervals here that are equivalent to one another:
- The augmented 6th (from Rule 3) is equivalent to the minor 7th (from Rule 1).
- The augmented 4th (from Rule 5) is equivalent to the diminished 5th (from Rule 4).

We can observe from the previous examples that:

- Both major and perfect intervals become augmented when increased by half step.
- The major intervals become minor when reduced by half step, and then become diminished when reduced by a further half step.
- The perfect intervals become diminished when reduced by half step.

The payoff for all this is that once you know all your intervals, you'll have a foolproof way of spelling all the chords you'll ever need. Hang in there!

INTERVALS IN MELODIES

Next we'll see how some of these intervals are used in well-known melodies. We'll start out with an excerpt from the jazz standard "All the Things You Are":

Notice this melodic phrase uses 4ths (perfect and augmented) and 2nds (major and minor), as well as some repeated notes in measures 3 and 5.

Jazz Standards

"All the Things You Are" is a great example of a *jazz standard*. Jazz standards are vocal tunes, generally written in the 1920s–1950s, that have very strong and enduring melodies. Successive generations of jazz musicians always "cut their teeth" on the standards.

Here are ten more jazz standards that all musicians and listeners should be acquainted with. Although pretty much everything else will most likely change over the next hundred years, it's a safe bet that these tunes will still be played by 22nd-century performers!

Johnny Mercer, "Autumn Leaves"
Johnny Green, "Body and Soul"
George Gershwin, "Our Love Is Here to Stay"
Bart Howard, "Fly Me to the Moon"
Bronisław Kaper, "On Green Dolphin Street"
Richard Rodgers, "My Romance"
Cole Porter, "Night and Day"
George Gershwin, "A Foggy Day"
Victor Young, "Stella by Starlight"
Erroll Garner, "Misty"

Photo provided by Photofest
George Gershwin

Next up we have an excerpt from the timeless pop song "Unchained Melody," recorded by many artists, including the Righteous Brothers:

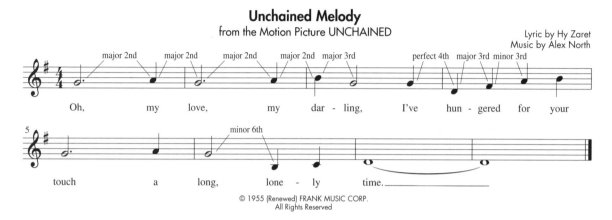

Unchained Melody
from the Motion Picture UNCHAINED

Lyric by Hy Zaret
Music by Alex North

The verse of this song starts out using major 2nds, moving to 3rds and 4ths in measures 3–4. A minor 6th is found in measure 6.

"Unchained Melody" (composed by Alex North) is one of the most recorded songs of the 20th century, with hundreds of versions in many different languages. Probably the most famous is the Righteous Brothers' recording from 1965, produced by Phil Spector. In the 1990s this version enjoyed a resurgence after being used in the hit movie *Ghost*. Elvis Presley also performed the song during his last television appearance in 1977.

Photo by GAB Archives/Redferns
Righteous Brothers

So now it's time to take a closer look at what makes a melody "tick." If you want to become a more informed listener, and/or you are writing your own melodies, here are some ground rules to be aware of:

MELODY CHARACTERISTICS

In the previous examples we have seen that melodies are created by combining intervals with rhythms. The melody is the musical "heart" of the song, the part that we can sing, hum, or whistle. While there is an infinite number of ways to combine intervals and rhythms, the following fundamentals commonly apply to well-known melodies across all styles.

Tonic: Most melodies will have a tonic (or "home base") that corresponds to the key that the song is in. The melody will often begin and/or end on this note, in order to sound resolved.

Motion: It's normal for melodies to have motion (i.e., move upward and downward in pitch, rather than staying on one note all the time); this generates interest for the listener.

Large vs. Small Intervals: Most of the intervals in vocal melodies tend to be small (i.e., 2nds or 3rds). This makes them more lyrical, as well as easier to sing. (These constraints will apply less if you are working in instrumental or jazz styles.) Larger melodic intervals (i.e., 5ths, 6ths, 7ths) are often followed by smaller intervals moving in the opposite direction.

Range: The majority of vocal melodies will have a *range* (distance from lowest to highest note) of around one octave, again to make them easier to sing. Instrumental melodies will often have a larger range (depending on the particular instrument used).

Sparse vs. Busier Rhythms: Contemporary melodies normally reflect the rhythmic subdivision and style of the song. For example, a rock song with an eighth-note feel would typically have eighth-note rhythmic figures in the melody, and an R&B ballad with a sixteenth-note feel would normally have sixteenth-note figures in the melody. For vocal melodies, it's best not to make the rhythms too busy, as this makes the melody harder to sing.

Repetition and Phrasing: Most classical and contemporary melodies are organized into phrases, which are often two, four, or eight measures in length. Longer phrases can be created by combining shorter ones. For example, you might come up with a two-measure *motif* (a short melodic phrase) to start your song. If you then repeat the same two-measure phrase with some alteration (to the melody and/or rhythm), you have created a four-measure phrase. The listener expects to hear some repetition, as it gives the song some structure and makes it easier to listen to. Too much repetition, however, may make the song monotonous. Let your ears be the judge!

We'll now take a closer look at some more well-known tunes, starting with simpler rhythms (whole, half, and quarter notes), and then move to some examples with eighth notes. All these examples are on the CD.

The Surprise Symphony

By Franz Joseph Haydn

A good example of rhythmic repetition! Measures 3–4 use the same rhythm as measures 1–2, but with different melody notes. In this way a four-measure phrase is created from an original two-measure motif. The melody uses triad arpeggios: For example, the C, E, and G in measures 1–2 outline a C major triad (more about triads and arpeggios in the next chapter).

Abide with Me

Words by Henry F. Lyte
Music by William H. Monk

"Abide with Me" is based on four-measure melodic and rhythmic phrases. The rhythm used in measures 1–4 is used again in measures 5–8, with melodic variations. The melody uses small intervals (2nds and 3rds), except for the larger perfect 5th in measure 2. We'll revisit this tune later when discussing counterpoint.

God Rest Ye Merry, Gentlemen

19th Century English Carol

Here is a good example of upward and downward motion in a melody. After the ascending perfect 5th in the first measure, we descend from B down to D using major and minor 2nds, then ascend back up to B using the same intervals in reverse. Simple but effective—and easy to sing!

Piano Concerto No. 2, First Movement Excerpt

By Sergei Rachmaninoff

This melody starts with a series of ascending intervals that range over an octave in just the first two measures. Then the melody begins to descend using a mix of 2nds and 3rds, and also adds some *chromatic* notes (i.e., notes not found within a certain key) in measure 4. There is not really any repetition here, so it feels like one long melodic phrase.

Careless Love

Anonymous

Note that, within these four-measure phrases, the first two measures have most of the rhythmic activity, while the last two measures just contain a whole note followed by a whole rest. This type of phrasing is used in many popular songs. Again, the same rhythms are used in measures 1–4 and 5–8.

Largo from Symphony No. 9
"New World"

By Antonín Dvořák

The "Symphony No. 9" excerpt is a great example of two-, four-, and eight-measure phrases. Note the rhythmic figure in measure 1, which is repeated for measure 2. However, the melody notes are different (E up to G in measure 1, and E–D–C in measure 2), thereby creating a two-measure phrase. Then between measures 3 and 4 we have rhythmic contrast, with two dotted-quarter/eighth-note pairs in measure 3, and a whole note in measure 4. Following on from measures 1–2, this yields a four-measure phrase. The notes and rhythms in measures 1–2 are then repeated for measures 5–6, and the rhythmic phrase in measures 3–4 is repeated during measures 7–8, but with different melody notes. This effectively creates an answering four-measure phrase in measures 5–8, which together with measures 1–4 produces an eight-measure phrase in total. The melody note in measure 4 is D, which sounds active in the key of C, giving the first four-measure phrase an unresolved feeling. By contrast, the melody note in measure 8 is C, which sounds restful or resolved in this key. See Chapter 12 for more on these concepts.

The Drunken Sailor

American Sea Chantey

This is another good example of different phrase lengths. Measures 1–2, 3–4, and 5–6 all use the same two-measure rhythmic phrase. Also, the melody notes in measures 1–2 are moved down (or *transposed*) by one scale degree to create the melody in measures 3–4, and these measures combine to make a four-measure phrase, overall. Also note the melodic variation within the two-measure phrases: Measures 1, 3, and 5 contain repeated single notes, whereas measures 2, 4, and 6 have more melodic movement using different intervals. Although measure 5 is a repeat of measure 1, measure 6 introduces new melodic material, leading into a different two-measure phrase in measures 7–8, which resolves to D, the tonic in the key of D *minor* (more about minor keys in Chapter 9). Measures 5–8, therefore, function as an answering four-measure phrase to measures 1–4.

CHAPTER 5

BASIC CHORDS AND PROGRESSIONS

> **What's Ahead:**
> - Creating three-note chords (triads)
> - Diatonic triads, progressions, and cadences
> - Triad inversions and voice leading
> - Triad arpeggios and suspensions

CREATING THREE-NOTE CHORDS (TRIADS)

Fasten your seat belts! We're now going to plunge into the fun world of chords. A *chord* is created when three or more notes are stacked on top of one another. A three-note chord is called a *triad*. Most contemporary styles are organized harmonically around chords. We'll now use some of the intervals developed in the last chapter to spell different triads, starting with the *major triad*.

You'll see that we've measured the intervals (major 3rd and perfect 5th) up from the *root* of the triad in each case. You'll remember (at least I hope you will) that these major and perfect intervals are found within the major scale, so this triad also consists of the 1st, 3rd, and 5th degrees of a C major scale.

Also note the letter "C" shown above the triad. This is our first example of a *chord symbol*. The chord symbol tells you which chord is contained in the measure.

A chord symbol consisting simply of a note name, with no additional suffix or description, indicates a major triad built from the note indicated. So the chord symbol "C" means a C major triad.

The major triad is the most basic and fundamental chord; it is used throughout pop and classical styles. Thus it is important to learn all of the major triads (not just C major).

If you have a piano or guitar handy, try playing through all of these major triads on your instrument. This will help you learn the sounds and shapes of the major triads in all keys.

Next up we have the minor triad, which we're also going to spell by using intervals.

Again, the intervals (this time minor 3rd and perfect 5th) are measured up from the root of the triad. When comparing this triad to the major triad, we see that the interval between the root and the middle note (or *third* of the chord) is now a minor 3rd instead of a major 3rd. So, another way this C minor triad can be derived is by taking the previous C major triad and lowering the third by a half step (in this case, E becomes E♭). This is true for all major triads: take any major triad, lower the third by a half step, and you will have a minor triad.

The chord symbol above the staff is now "Cm." There are two components to this chord symbol: the root ("C") and the suffix or description ("m"). A chord symbol consisting of a note name followed by the suffix "m" indicates a minor triad built from the note indicated. So the chord symbol "Cm" means a C minor triad.

The minor triad is used just about as widely as the major triad, so it's another good candidate for learning in all keys. Note the chord symbols above each chord.

Although the major and minor triads are the most common, there are two more triads that we sometimes use, which are the *augmented* and *diminished triads*.

These two new triads are shown above, so that we can compare them to the C major triad on the left.

- If we sharp the fifth of the C major triad, we get a C augmented triad. Note that there are two chord symbols above this chord—both the "+" and "aug" suffixes are commonly used to indicate an augmented triad.

- If we flat the third and fifth of the C major triad, we get a C diminished triad. Note that there are two chord symbols above this chord—both the "°" and "dim" suffixes are commonly used to indicate a diminished triad.

Play the C major triad on your piano or guitar, and then alter it to create the C minor, C augmented, and C diminished triads. Then try the same exercise, starting with different major triads.

DIATONIC TRIADS AND PROGRESSIONS

Let's define a couple of terms that will help you understand this section. *Diatonic* means "belong-ing to the major scale." Diatonic triads, therefore, are triads that are contained within a certain scale. Here are all of the triads contained within the C major scale:

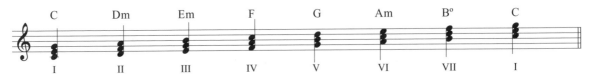

What we're doing here is building a triad from each note in the C major scale, making sure that all notes used are contained within the scale (if you're sitting at a piano, these triads use the white keys only, which make them pretty easy to find!). This process gives us the various triad *qualities* shown from left to right (major, minor, minor, major, major, minor, diminished, major).

A Roman numeral under the staff is a shorthand way of indicating chord function. In other words, we could say that within the key of C, a C major triad is a I chord, a D minor triad is a II chord, and so on. Throw this into the conversation when you next want to impress your musician friends!

Now we'll look at some songs that use diatonic triad progressions. A *chord progression* is simply a sequence of chords used in a song. This will also be our introduction to a leadsheet, which is a notated version of a song showing the melody and chord symbols (more details on charts and leadsheets can be found in Chapter 15).

Another new feature found in these next songs is the *pickup measure*. So far, in all of our song examples, the very first melody note has started on beat 1 of the first measure. "So what?" I hear you say, "Why wouldn't it?" Well, believe it or not, there are a lot of songs that start part-way into the first measure. We could write one or more rests at the beginning of the first measure to indi-cate this, but in practice composers normally use a pickup measure instead, which omits the rests at the beginning. So in the first measure of our next example, instead of the four beats we would expect in 4/4 time, there are only two sixteenth notes (equivalent to half a beat). This is a pickup measure, with the first melody note (G) falling on the "& of 4," or halfway through beat 4.

On to our first example of a diatonic triad progression, the Beatles' "Let It Be":

Let It Be

Words and Music by
John Lennon and Paul McCartney

Note the chord symbols placed above the staff, which fall on beats 1 and 3 of each measure. These are the chords used to accompany (or *harmonize*) the melody. Note that all of the chords are diatonic to the key of C (i.e., they are all contained in the series of triads on **Track 25**). If you are playing the song on a guitar or piano, you will play a part based on the chord symbols, and if you are playing bass, you will play a bass line that will normally include the root of each chord at the point of chord change (i.e., on beats 1 and 3 in this case).

It's a good exercise to figure out the function (i.e., Roman numeral) of each chord in this song by comparing it to the diatonic triads in the key of C. For example, the first triad is C (which is I in C), the next triad is G (which is V in C), and so on. The chords for many simpler songs can be analyzed this way, which helps when you're communicating with other players (as in, "Hey Nigel, that chorus is a VI–V–IV–I in C.").

Next up we have an excerpt from the well-known Cyndi Lauper song "Time After Time" (presented in leadsheet format):

Time After Time

Words and Music by
Cyndi Lauper and Rob Hyman

This example also uses a pickup measure: There are only three eighth notes (equivalent to one-and-a-half beats) in the first measure, so the first note lands on the "& of 3," or halfway through beat 3. Note the different chord rhythms (number of chords per measure) that occur: Most of the measures contain only one chord, but measures 3 and 7 each contain two chords, falling on beats 1 and 3. These chord rhythms are common across the range of contemporary pop and jazz styles. Again, note that all of the chords are diatonic to the key of C.

origins

"Time After Time" was the second single from Cyndi Lauper's *She's So Unusual* album, and is her second-most commercially successful song (after "Girls Just Want To Have Fun"). The song received a Grammy nomination in 1985 for "Song of the Year," and still shows up on adult contemporary radio playlists. The song has also been covered by over a hundred different artists, including Miles Davis, Willie Nelson, Matchbox 20, and Cassandra Wilson.

Photo by John Bellissimo

Cyndi Lauper

Although both of the previous examples were in the key of C, don't forget that all the other keys have diatonic triads too! For example, here are the diatonic triads in F major:

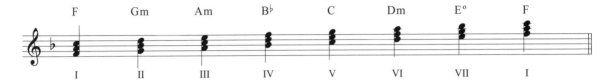

And here are the diatonic triads in G major:

Many famous songs use diatonic triads, so you should make it a goal to learn them in as many keys as possible!

TRIAD INVERSIONS AND VOICE LEADING

So far all of the chords we have developed have been in *root position*, meaning that the root of the chord has been on the bottom. This is the simplest way to write and to play a chord. However, as we start to combine chords together into progressions, we will need to start using *chord inversions*. This means having a note other than the root on the bottom. So instead of playing a triad root–third–fifth (from bottom to top), we might instead use third–fifth–root, or fifth–root–third. The reasons for doing this are:

- Inversions help us to *voice lead* or connect smoothly between chords, without unnecessary interval jumps.
- Inversions can be placed below a melody as a way to harmonize (or "flesh out") your arrangement.

Let's start with the C major triad, and invert it:

We'll define these different inversions of the C major triad as follows:

- The first triad is in root position (with the root on the bottom).
- The second triad is in first inversion (with the third on the bottom).
- The third triad is in second inversion (with the fifth on the bottom).
- The last triad is in root position, an octave higher than the first.

Earlier in this chapter we showed the root-position major triads in all keys. Now it's time to introduce the inversions of all these, starting with the first inversions:

And now here are the second inversion major triads:

Track 26
(0:26)

try this

> If you have a piano or guitar handy, try playing through all of these first- and second-inversion major triads on your instrument. These are very important chord shapes in all keys!

Now we'll go through the same process for minor triads, starting with the inversions of the C minor triad.

audio tracks 27

Here we have minor triads in root position, first inversion, second inversion, and finally root position again, from left to right. Now we'll present these minor triad inversions in all keys, starting with the first inversions:

Track 27
(0:07)

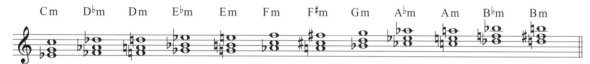

And now for the second inversion minor triads:

Track 27
(0:26)

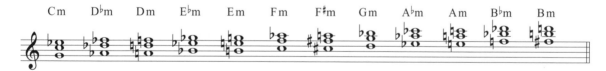

try this

> Once again, try playing through all of these if you have an instrument available.

Next we'll see how these triad inversions can be used to voice lead during a chord progression. The next example is a brief excerpt from Pachelbel's *Canon in D*, the most well-known work from the 17th-century composer Johann Pachelbel (shown here in the key of C).

Canon

By Johann Pachelbel

audio tracks 28

This is a piano adaptation of a work that was originally written for a quartet of stringed instruments. Note the chord symbols above the staff, describing the chords being used. Chord symbols are not normally written in classical music; however, we have added them here to illustrate that this is another diatonic triad progression. The root of each chord is played in the bass clef, and the upper triads are inverted to ensure smooth voice leading from left to right.

The triad inversions used in the treble-clef part can be analyzed as follows:

Measure 1: The C major triad on beat 1 is in second inversion, with the third of the chord (E) on top. The G major triad on beat 3 is in root position, with the fifth of the chord (D) on top.

Measure 2: The A minor triad on beat 1 is in second inversion, with the third of the chord (C) on top. The E minor triad on beat 3 is in root position, with the fifth of the chord (B) on top.

Measure 3: The F major triad on beat 1 is in second inversion, with the third of the chord (A) on top. The C major triad on beat 3 is in root position, with the fifth of the chord (G) on top.

Measure 4: The F major triad on beat 1 is in second inversion, with the third of the chord (A) on top. The G major triad on beat 3 is in second inversion, with the third of the chord (B) on top.

The top notes of these triads create a slow-moving melody, which in this case uses *scalewise movement* (i.e., major and minor 2nds) throughout.

One of the most-watched videos on YouTube is a rock guitar version of Pachelbel's *Canon*, which has been viewed over thirty million times! Originally the performer on the video was unknown, but he has since been identified as Jeong-Hyun Lim, a self-taught guitarist in South Korea. This video spawned many imitators, and a compilation video of the best guitar performances of the *Canon* (called *Ultimate Canon Rock*) has since been created.

SUSPENSIONS AND ROOT–FIFTH CHORDS

Going back to the major triad we built earlier, we can amend this triad by replacing the third of the chord with another note, or omitting it altogether. When we replace the third with another note, this is referred to as a *suspension*. When we omit the third, this is referred to as a *root–fifth* chord (or a "power chord" in rock music circles!). Here's an example of amending a C major triad in these various ways:

Let's compare these new chords to the C major triad shown on the left:

- If we replace the third of the C major triad with the second (D is the 2nd scale degree of the C major scale), we get the Csus2 chord. (The second of a chord can also be referred to as the ninth—see Chapter 11 for more information on chords with ninths.)
- If we replace the third of the C major triad with the fourth (F is the 4th scale degree of the C major scale), we get the Csus4 chord. (If you see a chord symbol that just says "Csus," then the Csus4 chord is assumed.)

- If we omit the third of the C major triad, we get the C5 chord. This chord can also be written as "C(no3rd)" or "C(omit 3rd)."

Both of the suspended chords sound active, and could resolve or move back to the C major triad (especially the Csus4 chord). The root–fifth chord has a transparent and powerful sound, and is commonly used in rock and metal styles. Next we will look at some examples of these new chords in action, beginning with an excerpt from the *Circle Dance* by Bartók, which uses suspended triads.

Circle Dance
from GYERMEKEKNEK (FOR CHILDREN)

By Béla Bartók

In this piano piece, the left-hand chords support the right-hand melody. Notice the Csus4 chords in measures 2 and 4, which then resolve back to C major triads.

Next up we have a modern rock example using sus2 and root–fifth chords: Train's "Drops of Jupiter (Tell Me)."

Drops of Jupiter (Tell Me)

Words and Music by Pat Monahan, Jimmy Stafford,
Rob Hotchkiss, Charlie Colin and Scott Underwood

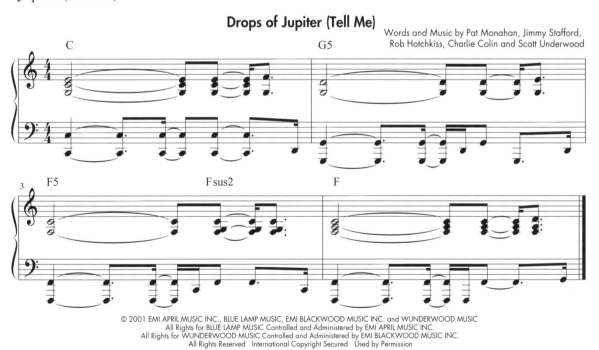

This piano groove uses sixteenth-note rhythms commonly found in modern rock and funk styles. (These styles are discussed more fully in Chapter 8.) Note the "G5" and "F5" chord symbols above the first beats of measures 2 and 3. These indicate that only the root and fifth of each chord are being used. Later in measure 3 (on the "& of 3") we see the "Fsus2" chord symbol, as the second of the F chord is now added to the root and fifth, resulting in the notes F–G–C. In actual practice, we would probably just show the "Fsus2" chord symbol for the whole measure, as all the notes in this measure are included within the Fsus2 (the separate chord symbols are shown here merely for your information). Measures 1 and 4 just use the regular major triad chord symbols "C" and "F."

Occasionally on major chords, the fourth is used in addition to, not instead of, the third. This chord can be written with the "add4" suffix (so a Cadd4 chord would include the notes E *and* F). This rather tense sound is used in our next example, which is the guitar intro to the classic rock song "All Right Now" by Free. This example will also introduce us to *tablature notation* (*tab*, for short) for the guitar. Tab notation shows the guitarist exactly where to place the fingers on the fretboard. This can come in handy when learning, since it is possible to play the same note in several different places on the guitar (as we saw in Chapter 1). This example shows the guitar tablature directly below the conventional music notation, which is a layout commonly used in guitar instruction and transcription books.

All Right Now

Words and Music by
Paul Rodgers and Andy Fraser

Let's look at the first A5 chord and compare the tab to the regular notation. On the treble clef, this stack of notes from bottom to top is A–E–A–E–A: the classic guitar power chord, with roots and fifths only. The tab notation shows where to play this on the fretboard: the "0" on the low-A string means to play this string open (not fretted), the "2" on the D and G strings means to fret each of these strings at the 2nd fret, and the "5" on the B and high-E strings means to fret each of these strings at the 5th fret. Note the "Dadd4" symbol on beat 1 of measure 3: This combines the third (F♯) and fourth (G) on the D chord. This then resolves to the D major triad on beat 3.

"All Right Now" remains one of Free's most recognizable and best-loved songs. It was a #1 single in the UK in 1970, and by 1990 it had received over one million radio plays in the U.S. The song has been resurrected for 21st-century audiences at concerts by Queen + Paul Rodgers. The song has also made it into several movie and TV soundtracks, including those of *American Beauty*, *Entourage*, and *The Sopranos*.

Photo provided by Photofest

Free

TRIAD ARPEGGIOS AND ALBERTI BASS

An *arpeggio* is simply a "broken chord." This means that, instead of playing the notes of a chord together, the notes are played one at a time, in succession. Guitarists and pianists will often play arpeggios when accompanying on a song. Piano players can use arpeggios in the left hand to accompany a melody played with the right hand. The following piano arrangement of "The Red River Valley" demonstrates a particular kind of arpeggio accompaniment known as *Alberti bass*, where the arpeggio pattern follows a specific note sequence: bottom–top–middle–top. This type of left-hand pattern is used in many styles, from rock ballads to Mozart piano sonatas.

The Red River Valley

Traditional American Cowboy Song

Note that we have used triad inversions in the left-hand pattern to voice lead smoothly from left to right. In measure 6, we used two different inversions (second, then first) on the B♭ major triad, so that the left-hand arpeggio did not collide with the right-hand melody.

> If you try playing this at the piano, make sure that the right-hand melody projects over the left-hand arpeggio pattern: Don't play the left-hand part too loudly in relation to the right-hand part.

CADENCES

A *cadence* is a series of chords that ends a section, or an entire piece. In classical terminology, a cadence is *strong* if it creates an impression of finality, and *weak* if this impression is not created. Following are examples of the four main types of cadences: *authentic*, *plagal*, *deceptive*, and *half*. Although these terms are not used in contemporary music theory, these progressions are nonetheless found across the range of contemporary styles, as well as in classical music.

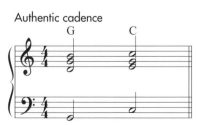

Authentic cadence

In the key of C, the previous example is a V–I diatonic-triad progression, which is considered the most final-sounding of all the cadences. Technically the version here would be called a *perfect* authentic cadence, as the root of each chord is in the bass clef, and the root of the tonic chord (C) is in the top voice. The use of different chord inversions would result in *imperfect* authentic cadences.

Track 32
(0:08)

In the key of C, this is a IV–I diatonic-triad progression. Although this still resolves strongly to the tonic chord, it is not considered as "final sounding" as the authentic cadence above. In classical pieces, this cadence is often used as a section ending, rather than as a final ending. This cadence is also known as the "Amen cadence," because of its frequent usage in hymns and church music.

Track 32
(0:13)

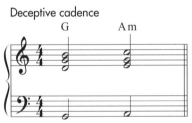

In the key of C, this is a V–VI diatonic-triad progression. A *deceptive* cadence moves from the V chord to a chord other than the I, or tonic, chord. The movement shown here (to the minor VI) is perhaps the most common of the various deceptive cadences. Here we have substituted the VI chord for the I chord (more about chord substitutions in Chapter 13).

Track 32
(0:18)

In the key of C, this is a IV–V diatonic-triad progression. A *half cadence* is technically any cadence ending on the V chord, but the IV–V is among the most common. This is considered the weakest type of cadence, as there is no resolution to the I chord.

From the standpoint of contemporary music theory and ear training, we can explain how these common progressions work in terms of the movement between active and resting tones within a major key. We will return to this important topic in Chapter 12!

Beyond the Basics

CHAPTER 6
MODAL, PENTATONIC, AND BLUES SCALES

What's Ahead:

- Modal scales and the relative major
- Melodic and harmonic use of modes
- Pentatonic, minor pentatonic, and blues scales

CREATING MODAL SCALES

Now we're going to head into the world of *modes*, or *modal scales*. A mode is simply the result of displacing another scale (i.e., starting the scale on a note other than the normal tonic or starting note). This displacement is most commonly done to a major scale, although it is also possible to create modes from other scales, as we will see later on. The use of modes is very common in contemporary pop and jazz styles. We'll start with the C major scale, that we built back in Chapter 3.

C major scale (also known as the C Ionian mode)

The regular, undisplaced major scale also has a modal name: the *Ionian mode*. So a song that just uses the major scale in the normal way (for example, the C major scale with the note C as the tonic) can be considered to be in the Ionian mode. The numbers below the staff indicate the major scale degrees being used.

If we then take this scale and displace it to start on various other scale degrees, we derive the other modal scales: *Dorian, Phrygian, Lydian, Mixolydian, Aeolian,* and *Locrian*. Note the numbers below each mode, showing which scale degrees have been altered (compared to a major scale built from the same starting note).

D Dorian mode (C major scale displaced to start on D)

Track 33 (0:07)

The major scale displaced to start on its 2nd degree is the *Dorian mode*. This mode has a minor sound due to the minor 3rd between the 1st and 3rd scale degrees, in this case D and F. Another way to derive this mode is to build a major scale from the same starting point (D major in this case), then flat the 3rd and 7th degrees. Dorian modes are found in folk, R&B/funk, and jazz styles.

E Phrygian mode (C major scale displaced to start on E)

Track 33
(0:14)

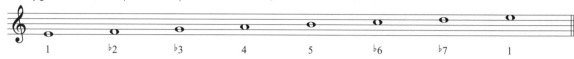

The major scale displaced to start on its 3rd degree is the *Phrygian mode*. This mode also has a minor sound due to the minor 3rd between the 1st and 3rd scale degrees, in this case E and G. It also has a more altered or dissonant quality due to the half step at the beginning (between E and F). Another way to derive this mode is to build a major scale from the same starting point (E major in this case), and flat the 2nd, 3rd, 6th, and 7th degrees. Phrygian modes are found in flamenco and Latin styles, as well as in jazz and fusion music.

F Lydian mode (C major scale displaced to start on F)

Track 33
(0:21)

The major scale displaced to start on its 4th degree is the *Lydian mode*. This mode has a major sound due to the major 3rd between the 1st and 3rd scale degrees, in this case F and A. It also has a bright and uplifting quality due to its ♯4 (B in this case). Another way to derive this mode is to build a major scale from the same starting point (F major in this case), and sharp the 4th degree. Lydian modes are widely used in TV and film music, as well as pop, rock, and jazz styles.

G Mixolydian mode (C major scale displaced to start on G)

Track 33
(0:28)

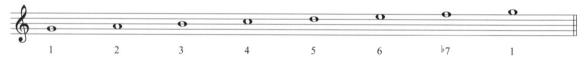

The major scale displaced to start on its 5th degree is the *Mixolydian mode*. This mode has a dominant sound due to the major 3rd between the 1st and 3rd scale degrees, and the minor 7th between the 1st and 7th scale degrees (much more about four-part dominant-seventh chords in the next chapter). Another way to derive this mode is to build a major scale from the same starting point (G major in this case), and flat the 7th degree. Mixolydian modes are an essential component of blues, blues/rock, and gospel styles.

A Aeolian mode (C major scale displaced to start on A)

Track 33
(0:35)

The major scale displaced to start on its 6th degree is the *Aeolian mode*. This mode has a minor sound due to the minor 3rd between the 1st and 3rd scale degrees, and is in fact the exact equivalent of the *natural minor scale* (more about minor scales in Chapter 9). Another way to derive this mode is to build a major scale from the same starting point (A major in this case), and flat the 3rd, 6th, and 7th degrees. Aeolian modes are a staple of contemporary pop, rock, and R&B styles.

B Locrian mode (C major scale displaced to start on B)

1 ♭2 ♭3 4 ♭5 ♭6 ♭7 1

The major scale displaced to start on its 7th degree is the *Locrian mode*. This mode also has a minor sound due to the minor 3rd between the 1st and 3rd scale degrees, and an altered or dissonant quality due to the half step at the beginning (between B and C in this case). This is also the only mode that does not have a perfect 5th above the tonic, which makes it less stable and useful. Another way to derive this mode is to build a major scale from the same starting point (B major in this case), and flat the 2nd, 3rd, 5th, 6th, and 7th degrees. Locrian modes tend to be limited to jazz and more experimental/fringe music styles.

RELATIVE MAJOR SCALE

In a modal context, the *relative major scale* is the scale that has been displaced to create the mode in question. So the relative major scale for all of the previous modal scale examples was C major. We will now use this idea to create a mode from a specific starting point, which will be helpful to you in real-world arranging and performance situations. So, for instance, if we had to create a C Dorian mode, we could ask ourselves: "Which major scale has C as its 2nd degree?" Using the whole and half steps from Chapter 3, we can figure out that C is the 2nd degree of a B♭ major scale. If we then displace the B♭ major scale to start on C, we have the C Dorian mode.

C Dorian mode (relative major: B♭)

1 2 ♭3 4 5 6 ♭7 1

In a similar way, we can create all of the other modal qualities starting on the note C, using a different relative major scale in each case.

C Phrygian mode (relative major: A♭)

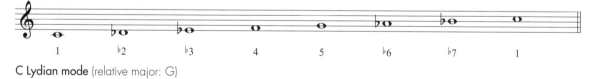

1 ♭2 ♭3 4 5 ♭6 ♭7 1

C Lydian mode (relative major: G)

1 2 3 ♯4 5 6 7 1

C Mixolydian mode (relative major: F)

1 2 3 4 5 6 ♭7 1

C Aeolian mode (relative major: E♭)

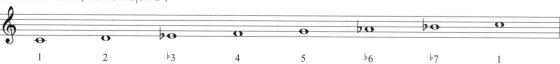

1 2 ♭3 4 5 ♭6 ♭7 1

C Locrian mode (relative major: D♭)

Track 34
(0:35)

1   ♭2   ♭3   4   ♭5   ♭6   ♭7   1

Ten Modal Hits You Should Know

The following well-known tunes use modal scales for their melodies:

Johannes Brahms, *Symphony No. 4*: Movement II
   (Phrygian)
R.E.M., "Man on the Moon" (Lydian)
The Beatles, "Norwegian Wood" (Mixolydian)
Judas Priest, "Painkiller" (Locrian)
Jean Sibelius, *Symphony No. 6* (Dorian)
Led Zeppelin, "Stairway to Heaven": guitar solo (Aeolian)
ABBA, "The Visitors" (Mixolydian)
Elmer Bernstein, *To Kill a Mockingbird* (Lydian)
"Twinkle, Twinkle, Little Star" (Ionian)
Jefferson Airplane, "White Rabbit" (Phrygian)

Jean Sibelius

Alternatively, you can still create these modes by altering a major scale built from the starting note, as shown by the numbers below each example. But the relative-major concept is very helpful for players, as they can think of each mode as a displaced version of a major scale that they already know—rather than having to learn a bunch of new scales from scratch!

MELODIC AND HARMONIC USE OF MODES

Now we'll take a closer look at how modes are used in some famous songs. Our first example is the main melodic riff from Glenn Frey's "The Heat Is On," which uses the C Mixolydian mode that we recently heard on **Track 34**. In general, we can say that a tune uses the C Mixolydian mode if the tonic is C, and if all the other notes used (including melody, bass line, and chords) are contained within C Mixolydian.

The Heat Is On
from the Paramount Motion Picture BEVERLY HILLS COP

Words by Keith Forsey
Music by Harold Faltermeyer

Note that this piano part establishes the root of C with a repetitive octave pattern in the left hand. (Yes, I know: The B♮s during beat 4 are not contained within C Mixolydian, but these are on a weak beat, and are used to connect back to the root (C) on beat 1—so for all intents and purposes we're still in C Mixolydian!) The well-known motif in the right hand makes prominent use of B♭, as well as other notes within the mode.

Note the key signature used for this example, which contains one flat (i.e., the key of F major). When you see a tonic in the music (C in this case) that does not appear to agree with the key signature, the use of a mode (C Mixolydian in this case) is the most likely reason. Some contemporary writers will prefer to indicate the tonic of the mode with the key signature, and then take care of any necessary accidentals in the music. In this case that would have meant a key signature of no sharps and flats (implying C as the tonic), with accidentals for the B♭s when they appeared. Modal music can be written either way, so be prepared!

Next we'll look at an excerpt from the Phil Collins song "In the Air Tonight," which is a great example of Aeolian melody and harmony. This will also be our introduction to *slash-chord* symbols, used when we need to place a chord over a particular bass note. In this case we're placing different chords over the note A in the bass. (Chapter 19 includes much more about different slash chords.) You'll remember from Chapter 3 that we derived the diatonic triads in C major (C, Dm, Em, F, G, Am, B°)—check out **Track 25**. Well, if we place these triads over the root A, we create an A Aeolian harmonic environment. In other words, all of the chords are contained within a C major scale (which is the relative major), and yet the note A is on the bottom. This is a common real-world application of modal harmony. The vocal melody also uses the A Aeolian mode. This example provides a simple piano accompaniment part on the bottom two staffs, and the vocal melody on the top staff.

In the Air Tonight

Words and Music by
Phil Collins

I can feel it com - in' in the air to - night ___ oh, Lord ___

Harmonically this example uses Am, G, and F triads (the VI, V, and IV diatonic triads from the key of C) over the repeated bass note of A. This tune is in the key of A minor (more about minor keys in Chapter 9).

"In the Air Tonight" is one of Phil Collins's best-known songs, and has been a staple on radio playlists since the 1980s. The song is noted for its atmospheric production and powerful drum sounds. The meaning of the song lyrics has been the subject of much speculation, and there are many rumors that the song is about the drowning death of a friend or family member, something that Collins has denied. The song was used for the pilot episode of *Miami Vice*, and this led to Collins himself acting in the hit TV series, in an episode entitled "Phil the Shill."

Photo by GAB Archives/Redferns

Phil Collins

Next up is a modal jazz tune by Miles Davis called "So What," which uses the D Dorian mode. In this tune the bass line (which is also the main melody, or *hook*) contains phrases that start and/or end on D. This bass line moves around a bit more than the previous "In the Air Tonight" example, but we still hear D as the tonic, and the bass line is wholly contained within D Dorian. The upper triads (G major and F major) are diatonic to the key of C, which is the relative major. So when we place these triads over the root D, we create a D Dorian harmonic environment.

So What

By Miles Davis

Harmonically this example uses the G and F triads (the V and IV diatonic triads from the key of C) over the bass line, which is centered around D. Again we are using slash chord symbols, this time G/D and F/D.

"So What" is the opening track on Miles Davis' landmark 1959 album, *Kind of Blue*, the best-selling jazz album of all time. The memorable piano and bass motif was written by Gil Evans, who collaborated with Davis on many recordings in the late '50s and early '60s. This recording epitomized the "cool jazz" movement that Davis was spearheading at the time, and remains a huge influence on jazz musicians to this day.

Photo by Marc Sharratt/CAMERA PRESS
Miles Davis

TRIAD PROGRESSIONS DIATONIC TO MODES

Now it's time to broaden our definition of modal harmony by including triad progressions that are diatonic to modes. In the preceding song examples, we related the upper triads to the bass line to determine the modal harmony being used. But what if we're looking at a song that just has a regular chord progression, with no repeated bass note or bass line? Well, we could *still* be using modal harmony, but we might have to dig a little deeper to find it! To help us understand the next example better, let's review the diatonic triads available in the key of A♭:

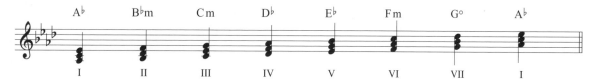

With these triads in mind, let's now look at one of the most famous triad arpeggio figures in 21st-century rock music, the intro to "Clocks," by Coldplay.

Clocks

Words and Music by Guy Berryman,
Jon Buckland, Will Champion and Chris Martin

This example uses arpeggios of E♭ major, B♭ minor, and F minor triads, and this chord structure is repeated throughout the song. Because all of these chords are included among the diatonic triads of A♭ major, you might be tempted to think that this is just another diatonic progression in A♭. But let's dig a little deeper.

- When a phrase like this keeps repeating, the ear attaches a lot of importance to the first measure in the phrase, as this is the strong measure. In other words, the E♭ chord that begins each four-measure phrase will sound like the tonic.

- To reflect this, notice that a key signature of three flats has been used, indicating that E♭ is the tonic. An accidental is therefore needed for the D♭ (the third of the B♭ minor triad) when it occurs in measures 2 and 3.

So we've ended up using triads diatonic to the A♭ major scale, but in a context where E♭ is our "home base." As E♭ is the 5th degree of the A♭ major scale, we can say that these triads are diatonic to E♭ Mixolydian. Here are the previously shown diatonic triads in A♭, now repositioned to start on E♭.

Track 35
(0:11)

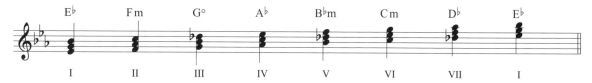

From this perspective, "Clocks" is using the I, V, and II triads within E♭ Mixolydian. Note that the V chord is minor within the Mixolydian mode—this is a very characteristic sound that contributes greatly to the tune's appeal!

"Clocks" was the most successful commercial hit from Coldplay's 2003 *A Rush of Blood to the Head* CD, winning a Grammy for "Record of the Year." It has been used in various TV shows and movies, including *ER*, *In America*, and *Confidence*. To date it has been the highest-selling song at Apple's iTunes music store.

Photo by David Atlas/Retna Ltd.
Coldplay

PENTATONIC SCALE

Now it's time to look at some other scales, beginning with the *pentatonic scale*. This is a five-note scale used across a range of pop and jazz styles. It can be derived by taking the major scale and removing the 4th and 7th degrees.

audio tracks 36

C pentatonic

From bottom to top, this scale contains the following intervals: whole step–whole step–minor 3rd–whole step–minor 3rd. Many famous tunes have been created from this scale, as its combination of whole steps and minor 3rds has an inbuilt melodic quality. One of many examples of this is the following excerpt from the song "Will the Circle Be Unbroken," popularized by the Nitty Gritty Dirt Band, among others. The tune uses the E pentatonic scale (an E major scale without the 4th and 7th degrees: E–F♯–G♯–B–C♯).

Will the Circle Be Unbroken

Words by Ada R. Habershon
Music by Charles H. Gabriel

Track 36
(0:06)

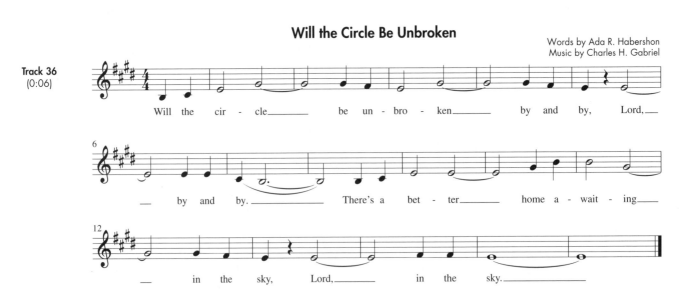

MINOR PENTATONIC SCALE

Next up is the *minor pentatonic scale*. This can be considered a mode of the pentatonic scale and is sometimes referred to as the "blues pentatonic." If we displace the previous C pentatonic scale to start on A instead of C, we get the following A minor pentatonic scale:

A minor pentatonic

Track 36
(0:39)

From bottom to top, this scale contains the following intervals: minor 3rd–whole step–whole step–minor 3rd–whole step. This scale is widely used in rock, funk, and R&B songs, including the Stevie Wonder classic "Superstition," which uses an E♭ minor pentatonic scale (E♭–G♭–A♭–B♭–D♭).

Superstition

Words and Music by
Stevie Wonder

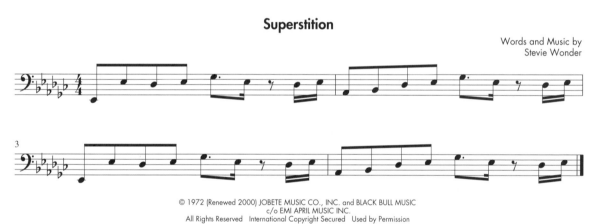

© 1972 (Renewed 2000) JOBETE MUSIC CO., INC. and BLACK BULL MUSIC
c/o EMI APRIL MUSIC INC.
All Rights Reserved   International Copyright Secured   Used by Permission

BLUES SCALE

Lastly, we'll see how to derive the *blues scale* by adding one note (the ♭4 or ♭5) to the minor pentatonic scale. For example, if we take the A minor pentatonic scale and add the connecting tone D♯ between D and E, we create an A blues scale.

A blues

Track 36
(0:46)

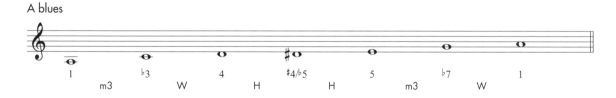

The blues scale is widely used in blues styles (of course!), as well as in rock, gospel, and R&B. Here's an excerpt from Deep Purple's powerful guitar anthem "Smoke on the Water," which is based on a G blues scale (G–B♭–C–D♭–D–F):

Smoke on the Water

Words and Music by Ritchie Blackmore,
Ian Gillan, Roger Glover, Jon Lord and Ian Paice

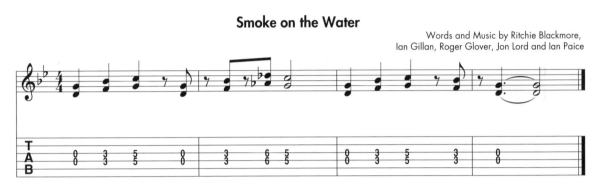

Tablature notation again is shown directly below the conventional music staff. This is a series of inverted power chords on the guitar, with the root on the top and the fifth on the bottom. For example, on beat 1 in the first measure, the root (G) is on the top and the fifth (D) is on the bottom. Such two-note voicings (perfect 4ths in this case) are also sometimes referred to as *dyads*. The top notes of this riff (G, B♭, C, and so on) are derived from the G blues scale. Rock on!

CHAPTER 7
FOUR-PART CHORDS AND PROGRESSIONS

What's Ahead:

- Creating four-part chords
- Diatonic four-part chords and progressions
- Four-part chord inversions and voice leading
- Four-part chord arpeggios and Alberti bass
- Four-part chord alterations

CREATING FOUR-PART CHORDS

Following on from the basic triads explained in Chapter 5, we're now going to derive some *four-part chords* (i.e., chords containing four notes). Most four-part chords are *seventh chords*, in which the fourth note of the chord is the interval of a 7th above the root. The most common four-part chords used in pop and jazz styles are the *major seventh, major sixth, minor seventh, minor seventh with flatted fifth* (also called *half-diminished seventh*), *minor sixth, minor/major seventh, dominant seventh, suspended dominant seventh,* and *diminished seventh* chords. As before, we will build each chord up from the root, using specific intervals as follows:

These chords are formed by building the following intervals above the root:

- major seventh chord: major 3rd, perfect 5th, major 7th
- major sixth chord: major 3rd, perfect 5th, major 6th
- minor seventh chord: minor 3rd, perfect 5th, minor 7th
- minor seventh with flatted fifth chord: minor 3rd, diminished 5th, minor 7th
- minor sixth chord: minor 3rd, perfect 5th, major 6th
- minor/major seventh chord: minor 3rd, perfect 5th, major 7th
- dominant seventh chord: major 3rd, perfect 5th, minor 7th
- suspended dominant seventh chord: perfect 4th, perfect 5th, minor 7th
- diminished seventh chord: minor 3rd, diminished 5th, diminished 7th

Note that each chord symbol consists of a root note ("C" in this case) followed by a suffix.

Some chord symbols have just a letter name and a number (i.e., the C6 and C7 chords above). In this case, if the number is less than "7," the chord has a major quality; and if the number is "7" or greater, the chord has a dominant quality, and is therefore likely to lead back to a tonic chord. (More about dominant chords later on.)

Chord symbols can be confusing if you're not careful! Notice that some of the new chords we have just created have the same names as some intervals we defined back in Chapter 4. For instance, the first chord in the previous example is a major seventh chord, which contains the interval of a major 7th from the root up to the seventh. This will not be problem, provided you are always clear whether your terminology refers to a chord or an interval. This is particularly important when the chord name does not correspond to the largest interval within the chord. For example, a minor sixth chord actually contains the interval of a major 6th from the root up to the sixth—again, no problem if you keep a "firewall" in your mind, separating chord names from interval names!

Some other points to be aware of regarding these chords:

- The sixth chord symbol ["Cm(maj7)"] looks rather unusual, as the suffix refers to both minor and major. The minor part ("m") refers to the minor 3rd (C up to E♭), and the major part ("maj") refers to the major 7th (C up to B). This rather tense-sounding chord is commonly used in jazz styles.

- The suspended dominant seventh chord (C7sus4), is a dominant seventh chord in which the third (E) has been replaced by the fourth (F). This is similar to how we created suspended triads back in Chapter 5. The suspended dominant is a common sound in modern pop music styles.

- Note that most of these chords (except for the minor seventh with flatted fifth and diminished seventh) contain a perfect 5th above the root. The perfect 5th does not contribute to the definition of the chord (i.e., it does not help our ear make the distinction between different four-part chords). Rather, it is the third and seventh (or sixth) of the chord that define each chord quality.

DIATONIC FOUR-PART CHORDS AND PROGRESSIONS

Now it's time to see how some of these four-part chords fit into different major keys. Do you remember when we found out about the triads living in major keys (the diatonic triads in Chapter 5)? Well, we're about to do the same thing with four-part chords. Here are the diatonic four-part chords contained within the C major scale.

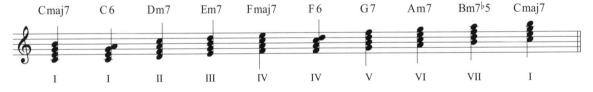

What we're doing here is building a four-part chord from each note in the C major scale, making sure that all notes used are contained with the scale (which, in the key of C, means we are using just the white keys on the piano again). This gives us the various chord qualities shown here from left to right (major seventh/major sixth, minor seventh, minor seventh, major seventh/major sixth, dominant seventh, minor seventh, minor seventh with flatted fifth). Note that the 1st and 4th scale degrees each have two chords built from them: Both the major seventh and major sixth chords. As with the diatonic triads, a lot of songs are written using these diatonic four-part chords.

The Roman numeral under the staff again indicates chord function. In other words, we could say that within the key of C, both the Cmaj7 and C6 chords are I chords, the Dm7 is a II chord, and so on. (More ways to impress your musician friends…) Of course, we can have diatonic four-part chords in any key, not just in C major! In this chapter we'll derive the four-part chords within a couple more keys, starting with D major.

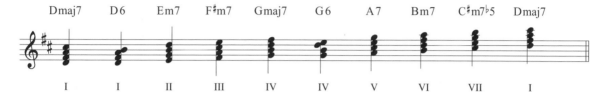

Next we'll look at an excerpt that uses a diatonic four-part chord progression in the key of D major. This is from the classic Motown pop song "Heatwave," made famous by Martha and the Vandellas in the 1960s. Here the verse of the song is presented as a leadsheet, showing the melody and chord symbols.

Heatwave (Love Is Like a Heatwave)

Words and Music by Edward Holland,
Lamont Dozier and Brian Holland

Note the chord symbols placed above the staff, which fall on beat 1 of each measure (with each Bm7 chord lasting for two measures). These are the chords used to harmonize the melody. Note that all of the chords are diatonic to the key of D (i.e., they are all contained in the series of four-part chords on **Track 38**). Again, it's a good exercise to figure out the function (i.e., Roman numeral) of each chord by comparing it to the diatonic four-part chords in the key of D. For example, the first chord is Em7 (which is II in D), the next chord is F♯m7 (which is III in D), and so on.

In preparation for the next section on four-part chord inversions and voice leading, we'll now derive diatonic four-part chords in the key of A major:

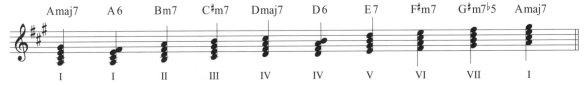

FOUR-PART CHORD INVERSIONS AND VOICE LEADING

Next we'll use some of these diatonic chords in A major to demonstrate how four-part chords can be inverted (in a similar way to the triad inversions in Chapter 5). Here are the inversions of an Amaj7 chord (a tonic, or I, chord in the key of A major).

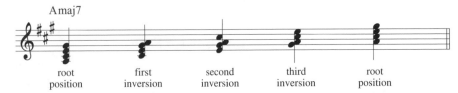

We'll define these different inversions of the A major seventh chord as follows:

- The first chord is in root position (with the root on the bottom).
- The second chord is in first inversion (with the third on the bottom).
- The third chord is in second inversion (with the fifth on the bottom).
- The fourth chord is in third inversion (with the seventh on the bottom).
- The last chord is in root position, an octave higher than the first.

Now we'll go through the same process for the Bm7 and E7 chords (the II and V chords in A major):

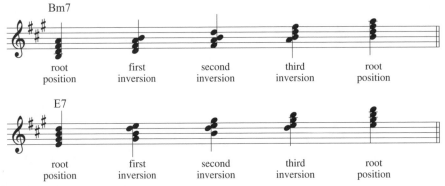

Next we'll look at a diatonic four-part chord progression in A major, seeing how it benefits from inversions and voice leading. Listen to **Track 40** to hear a series of four-part chords in root position, all diatonic to the key of A.

Notice how the previous example sounds rather disjointed, because we are jumping around in root position. But with the use of inversions, this progression can be made smoother and more musical. Listen to **Track 40** to hear inversions and voice leading applied to these four-part chords.

We will next use these inverted four-part chords to harmonize an excerpt from the classic R&B/pop song "This Will Be (an Everlasting Love)." This will also give us our first sneak peek at *triplets*, which will be explored further in the next chapter. *Triplets* are used to squeeze three rhythmic units (usually quarter or eighth notes) into the space normally occupied by two. For example, the first measure starts out with a quarter rest followed by two quarter notes, all under a triplet sign. This shows that these three events (which would normally occupy three beats) occupy only two beats, with each note and rest lasting for two-thirds of a beat. Similarly, the second measure starts with a quarter rest followed by an eighth note, again under a triplet sign. This squeezes these two events (which would normally occupy one-and-a-half beats) into one beat, with the rest lasting for two-thirds of a beat, and the note lasting for one-third of a beat.

This Will Be (An Everlasting Love)

Words and Music by
Marvin Yancy and Chuck Jackson

"This Will Be (an Everlasting Love)" was Natalie Cole's debut single in 1975. The song became one of her greatest hits, winning her a Grammy for "Best R&B Vocal Performance." It remains a staple on many radio playlists, especially for adult contemporary and smooth jazz stations. A few years ago the song enjoyed a new life as the theme song on TV ads for a well-known online dating service. It has also appeared in various movies, including *The Parent Trap* and *While You Were Sleeping*.

Photo by Charlie Gillett Archives/Redferns
Natalie Cole

FOUR-PART CHORD ARPEGGIOS AND ALBERTI BASS

Back in Chapter 5 we created arpeggios from triads, and now it's time to do this using four-part chords. In the recording of "The Red River Valley" on **Track 31**, we used an Alberti-bass pattern for the left-hand arpeggios. The following excerpt from Diabelli's *Sonatina in F, Op. 168 #1* has a similar left-hand pattern, now mixing in some four-part chords with triads.

Sonatina in F, Op.168 #1

By Anton Diabelli

In measure 3 the bass-clef part outlines a C7 chord, and in the last half of measure 7 the bass-clef part (together with the B♮ in the treble clef) outlines a G7 chord.

Note that this example also contains some articulation markings: *slurs* (curved lines joining groups of notes, indicating a smooth and connected playing style) and *staccato dots* (indicating a short and separated playing style). You'll find more about different articulations in the next chapter.

Apart from the two four-part chords mentioned above, all of the bass-clef patterns use triad arpeggios. See if you can figure out which triads are being used in each measure. Refer back to Chapter 5 as needed.

Anton Diabelli was a noted Austrian music publisher, editor, and composer. In the early 19th century, he became known through his beginner-friendly arrangements of popular piano pieces. His publishing company was the first to publish works by the up-and-coming Franz Schubert. Diabelli composed the waltz on which Beethoven wrote his remarkable set of *Diabelli Variations*.

Anton Diabelli

FOUR-PART CHORD ALTERATIONS

We conclude this chapter by exploring alterations to some four-part chords, where the fifth of the chord has been raised or lowered by a half step. We have seen one example of this already: The minor seventh with flatted fifth chord is an altered version of the minor seventh chord. Now we'll see that the fifth can be raised or lowered on major seventh, minor seventh, and dominant seventh chords.

These alterations can be summarized as follows:

Major seventh chords: In measure 2, the fifth is lowered by half step to G♭, creating the Cmaj7♭5 chord.

In measure 3, the fifth is raised by half step to G♯, creating the Cmaj7♯5 chord.

Minor seventh chords: In measure 5, the fifth is lowered by half step to G♭, creating the Cm7♭5 chord.

In measure 6, the fifth is raised by half step to G♯, creating the Cm7♯5 chord.

Dominant seventh chords: In measure 8, the fifth is lowered by half step to G♭, creating the C7♭5 chord.

In measure 9, the fifth is raised by half step to G♯, creating the C7♯5 chord.

These altered chords are commonly found in jazz, as well as in more harmonically-advanced R&B styles.

CHAPTER 8

MORE NOTATION AND RHYTHMIC CONCEPTS

What's Ahead:

- Eighth-note rhythmic feels and triplets
- Sixteenth-note rhythmic feels and triplets
- Tempo and dynamic markings
- Slurs and articulations
- More time signatures

EIGHTH-NOTE RHYTHMIC FEELS AND TRIPLETS

Most music styles use either an eighth-note or a sixteenth-note rhythmic subdivision, or "feel," meaning that the smallest regularly occurring rhythmic unit is either an eighth or sixteenth note. In contemporary styles, each of these subdivisions can be played either *straight* or *swing*. The swing feels require the use of triplets, at either the eighth- or sixteenth-note level—but let's wait a bit before we get to that.

We'll start out with the simplest rhythmic feel, which is *straight eighths*. In a straight-eighths feel, each eighth note is of equal length and divides the beat exactly in half.

Straight eighth notes

Note the rhythmic counting below the staff. This is how eighth-note rhythms are normally counted, with the "1," "2," "3," and "4" falling on the downbeats, and the "&" falling halfway in between, on the upbeats.

Many pop and rock songs use a straight-eighths feel, including John Cougar Mellencamp's "Hurts So Good." In contemporary styles, the drummer is typically responsible for defining the rhythmic feel, so we're now going to look at the drum part for the chorus of this song. This is our first look at a *drum chart*, where lines and spaces on the staff (instead of designating actual pitches, as in piano or guitar notation) represent different elements within the drumkit. Note the legend provided; this indicates which line or space corresponds to which part of the drumkit. In order to be as clear as possible, it is always advisable when writing drum charts to provide a key of this sort. This drum legend shows the following elements of the drumkit:

- BD (bass drum):   Normally based around beats 1 and 3 in most pop, rock, and R&B.

- SD (snare drum):   Normally on beats 2 and 4 (the backbeats) in most pop, rock, and R&B.

- HH (hi-hat):   Normally outlines the rhythmic subdivision (either eighths or sixteenths)

- TT 1, 2, 3 (three tom-toms):   Tuned to different pitches; used for fills or emphasis.

- Crash (crash cymbal):   Played on strong downbeats and beginnings of sections (often following a fill).

The bass drum (also known as the kick drum) is usually written in the bottom space on the drum staff, and the snare drum is usually written in the second space from the top. However, the placement of the other elements of the drumkit is rather non-standardized—which is why it's good to provide a legend!

Back at the beginning of this chapter we spoke about downbeats and upbeats. If we play on an upbeat and then rest (or sustain) through the following downbeat, this results in an *anticipation*, which is a vital rhythmic element in contemporary styles. We see this concept at work in the intro to Deep Purple's, hard-driving, "Space Truckin'," which has a straight-eighths feel. In the first measure of this drum chart, the bass drum and cymbal land on the "& of 1," "& of 3," and "& of 4" (i.e., halfway through beats 1, 3, and 4), with nothing landing on the following downbeats. This is a great example of rhythmic anticipation:

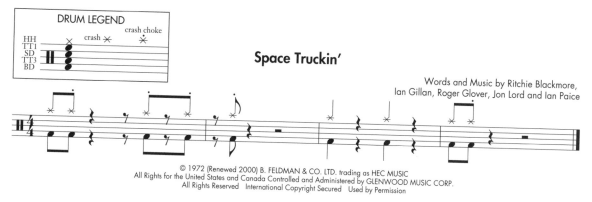

You'll find that the drum legend has some additional drumkit elements this time, including a *crash choke*, where the drummer immediately grabs the crash cymbal after playing it, so that it does not ring (indicated in the notation with a dot).

Continuing with the drum part for "Space Truckin'," we'll now look at the chorus, in which Deep Purple drummer, Ian Paice, makes interesting use of downbeats and upbeats. Here the snare drum is playing all of the downbeats, alternating with the bass drum playing upbeats on the "& of 3" and the "& of 4," creating a very cool syncopated effect.

Space Truckin'

Ten More Deep Purple Songs You Should Know

Deep Purple has a solid place in rock music history, and the band is still active in the 21st century. Most of their best-known songs were written and recorded in the 1970s, and incorporate classical, blues, and jazz elements into a unique hard-rocking style. Here are ten more of their songs that you should check out:

- "Speed King"
- "Child in Time"
- "Fireball"
- "Strange Kind of Woman"
- "Highway Star"
- "Maybe I'm a Leo"
- "Smoke on the Water"
- "Lazy"
- "Woman from Tokyo"
- "Rat Bat Blue"

Photo provided by Photofest

Deep Purple

On to our next rhythmic feel, *swing eighths*. In a swing-eighths feel, the second eighth note of each beat (the "&" in the rhythmic counting) lands two-thirds of the way through the beat. This is equivalent to playing on the first and third parts of an eighth-note triplet. As we saw in the last chapter, triplet signs are used to fit three rhythmic units (in this case, eighth notes) into the space normally occupied by two. So within each quarter-note/eighth-note triplet in the second measure below, the quarter note will land on the downbeat, and the eighth note will land two-thirds of the way through the beat. In contemporary styles, musicians might apply a swing-eighths interpretation, where appropriate, to regular eighth notes (as notated in the first measure below), or this rhythmic feel may be indicated specifically (as in the second measure). In that case, these two measures become functionally equivalent.

Swing eighth notes

Track 43
(0:09)

Next we'll look at an excerpt from a fun song by ABBA that uses a swing-eighths feel, "Waterloo." This is presented in leadsheet format, with melody and chord symbols. The notation just shows regular eighth notes; we need to interpret them as swing eighths in order to sound like the record.

Waterloo

Words and Music by Benny Andersson,
Bjorn Ulvaeus and Stig Anderson

Wa - ter-loo, I____ was de - feat - ed, you won____ the war.

Wa - ter-loo, prom - ise to love____ you for - ev - er more.

There will also be times when we need to land on all three parts of an eighth-note triplet. In this case, the swing-eighths rhythmic interpretation will not work, as this only allows us to access the first and third parts of the triplet. Instead, we either need to use eighth-note triplet signs in 4/4 time, or use *12/8 time*, which exposes all of the eighth notes without the need for triplet signs. The following example shows these two different types of notation:

Eighth-note triplets vs. 12/8 time

Track 43
(0:17)

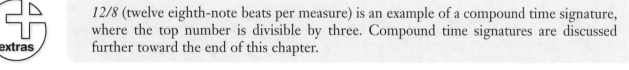

extras

12/8 (twelve eighth-note beats per measure) is an example of a compound time signature, where the top number is divisible by three. Compound time signatures are discussed further toward the end of this chapter.

In the first measure above, each beat is divided into three equal parts. In the second measure, the time signature allows for twelve eighth notes in the measure, but we still hear four "big beats," one at the start of each beamed group of eighth notes. These two measures are therefore functionally equivalent. As a general rule, I would suggest notating in 4/4 time unless there are a lot of eighth-note triplet signs needed, in which case it may be less cumbersome to notate in 12/8 time.

Our next example is the famous Whitney Houston ballad "Saving All My Love for You," which has an eighth-note triplet feel. We have a choice as to how to notate it: either in 4/4 with triplet signs, or in 12/8. Following is a leadsheet for this song, notated both ways so you can compare.

First we have the 4/4 version:

And now the 12/8 version:

There are some chord symbols in "Saving All My Love for You" that we haven't seen before.

- The Bm9 chord is a larger form of the Bm7 chord. Five-part chords like this are explained in Chapter 11.

- The D/E is a slash chord symbol, and indicates a D major triad placed over E in the bass, creating a larger form of an E7sus4 chord. Information about slash chords and upper-structure voicings can be found in Chapter 19.

- The B/F♯ is another slash chord symbol, meaning a B major triad with its fifth (F♯) in the bass.

"Saving All My Love for You" was the second single from Whitney Houston's debut album, topping the charts in both the US and UK. The song won the 1986 Grammy award for "Best Female Pop Vocal Performance." Houston's acting role in the movie *Waiting to Exhale* is reflective of the character she portrays in this song.

Photo © Photofest

Whitney Houston

SIXTEENTH-NOTE RHYTHMIC FEELS AND TRIPLETS

Now we'll look at rhythms using sixteenth notes. In a sixteenth-note feel, all the eighth-note upbeats ("&"s) will fall exactly halfway between the downbeats. Additionally, each eighth-note must now be subdivided in a manner that determines the rhythmic feel. In a *straight-sixteenths* feel, each sixteenth note is of equal length and divides the eighth-note exactly in half (and the beat exactly into quarters).

See the rhythmic counting below the staff; this is how sixteenth-note rhythms normally are counted. In between the beat numbers ("1," "2," "3," "4") and the "&"s, we have "e" on the second sixteenth note within each beat, and "a" on the fourth sixteenth note within each beat.

Many R&B, funk, and modern rock songs use a straight-sixteenths feel, including the funk/rock favorite "Another One Bites the Dust" by Queen. Here we'll take a look at the bass part for the verse of this song, which includes tablature as well as regular notation. Because the bass has four strings, there are four lines on the bass-tab staff. The treble-clef staff on top contains the vocal melody.

Another One Bites the Dust

Words and Music by
John Deacon

On to our next rhythmic feel, *swing sixteenths*. In a swing-sixteenths feel, the second and fourth sixteenth notes in each beat (the "e" and "a" in the rhythmic counting) land two-thirds of the way through their respective halves of the beat. This is equivalent to playing on the first and third parts of a sixteenth-note triplet. In contemporary styles, musicians might apply a swing-sixteenths interpretation, where appropriate, to regular sixteenth notes (as notated in the first measure below), or this rhythmic feel may be indicated specifically (as in the second measure). In that case, these two measures become functionally equivalent.

Track 43
(0:36)

Next we'll look at an excerpt from "We're in This Love Together," a song made famous by Al Jarreau that uses a swing-sixteenths feel. This is given in leadsheet format, with melody and chord symbols. The notation uses regular sixteenth notes—which we need to interpret as swing sixteenths in order to sound like the record.

We're in This Love Together

Words and Music by
Keith Stegall and Roger Murrah

© 1980 EMI BLACKWOOD MUSIC INC. and UNIVERSAL MUSIC - CAREERS
All Rights Reserved   International Copyright Secured   Used by Permission

There are some more new slash chord symbols in "We're in This Love Together":

- The Cm7/F means a C minor seventh chord placed over F in the bass, creating a larger form of an F7sus4 chord.
- The G♭/A♭ means a G♭ major triad placed over A♭ in the bass, creating a larger form of an A♭7sus4 chord.

Another approach to notating a swing-sixteenths feel is to multiply all of the rhythmic values by two and notate it in swing eighths. In this case, there would be only two beats, or pulses, per measure (each of which would be a half note), and there would be twice the number of measures.

Charts like this often have the directions "in 2" or "2 feel" written at the top. Strictly speaking, such charts should use the 2/2 time signature, indicating that there are two half-note beats per measure (more about different time signatures later in this chapter). However, in fake books, I do sometimes see this done using the normal 4/4 time signature, so be prepared. Here's an example of the same excerpt, now using eighth notes in a "2 feel":

We're in This Love Together

There will also be times when we need to land on all three parts of a sixteenth-note triplet. In this case, the swing-sixteenths rhythmic interpretation will not work; instead, we need to use triplet signs to indicate the sixteenth-note triplets.

Sixteenth-note triplets

Track 43
(0:46)

It is unusual for contemporary styles to use all of the sixteenth-note triplet subdivisions in each measure. More commonly, sixteenth-note triplets will be used in part of the measure as embellishment. Our next example is the intro drum part to the Beatles classic "Come Together," probably one of the most famous examples of sixteenth-note triplets ever recorded.

Come Together

Words and Music by
John Lennon and Paul McCartney

Notice that Ringo Starr plays triplets on the hi-hat during the first half of beat 2, then on the toms during beat 3 and the first half of beat 4. In total, half of each measure uses sixteenth-note triplets.

Everything You've Ever Wanted To Know About "Come Together"

"Come Together" was released in October 1969 as the B-side to the George Harrison song, "Something." It was also the opening track on the Beatles album *Abbey Road*. Although credited to Lennon/McCartney, the song was written mainly by John Lennon.

A lawsuit was filed against Lennon by Chuck Berry's music publisher, Morris Levy, claiming that part of the "Come Together" lyric was very similar to the Berry song "You Can't Catch Me." The suit was settled out of court, and Lennon subsequently recorded several songs in Levy's catalog.

In the UK, the song was banned for a while by the BBC, on the grounds that the mention of "Coca Cola" in the lyric was a reference to drugs.

The song has been covered by many artists, including Aerosmith, Michael Jackson, Tina Turner, Joe Cocker, Michael Ruff, and Soundgarden.

Photo provided by Photofest

The Beatles

TEMPO AND DYNAMIC MARKINGS

So, I hear you ask: "Now that we know about these rhythmic subdivisions and feels, how do we know how fast to play a piece of music?" Good question! The speed of a piece of music is referred to as the *tempo* (another one of those Italian words). In contemporary styles, the tempo is often indicated exactly on the score, as the number of beats per minute (abbreviated "BPM"). In the following pop ballad, the tempo marking says "♩ = 65"; this means that there are sixty-five beats per minute.

Ballad tempos are normally in the 50–70 BPM range. Examples of other style tempos are smooth jazz (80–110), pop/rock (110–140), and bebop jazz (180 and up).

In classical music, it is typical to indicate the tempo range using Italian terms. For example, Haydn's "The Heavens Are Telling" (from the oratorio *The Creation*) is marked "Allegro," which generally refers to a relatively fast tempo.

The Heavens Are Telling
from THE CREATION

By Franz Joseph Haydn

Track 44
(0:20)

When the tempo range of a piece is indicated in this way, the exact tempo is left to the player's discretion.

extras

A *metronome* is a piece of equipment that produces a tick (and/or flashes a light) for each beat at the specified tempo. Your local music store will have a selection of metronomes, both *mechanical* (using a pendulum) and digital (computerized). The tempo (or number of beats per minute) is also referred to as a "metronome mark."

Tempo Markings You Should Know

- Largo or Lento: very slow (40–60 BPM)
- Adagio: slow and stately (60–76 BPM)
- Andante: at a walking pace (76–108 BPM)
- Moderato: moderately (108–120 BPM)
- Allegro: fast and bright (120–140 BPM)
- Vivace: lively and fast (140–168 BPM)
- Presto: very fast (168–200 BPM)

Some Common Qualifiers

- molto: much or very (e.g., Allegro molto = very fast and bright)
- non troppo: not too much (e.g., Allegro non troppo = fast, but not too fast)
- con brio: with vigor or spirit (e.g., Allegro con brio = fast, with vigor)

Most pieces of music (especially in contemporary styles) keep the same tempo throughout. However, some pieces will slow down or speed up at different times. The most common ways to indicate a gradual slow-down or speed-up in the tempo is to use the Italian terms *ritardando* (abbreviated *rit.*) and *accelerando* (abbreviated *accel.*), respectively. Sometimes it is also necessary to pause, or hold a note for a period of time, before resuming with the tempo; this is done with a *fermata*. A fermata will often be used following a slowing of the tempo, as in the following example:

Track 44
(0:30)

rit. -

Listening to **Track 44** (section starting 0:30), you can hear that the tempo gradually slows in measure 2, before pausing at the fermata (the sign above the whole note in measure 3).

Next we'll look at *dynamic markings*, which tell the performer how softly or loudly to play. The two main dynamic indications used in music are *p* (*piano*, meaning soft) and *f* (*forte*, meaning loud). These can be modified by the prefix *m* (for *mezzo*, or medium), as in *mp* (medium soft) and *mf* (medium loud). Beyond *p* (for soft), we can use *pp* (*pianissimo*, meaning very soft) and *ff* (*fortissimo*, meaning very loud). We can go even further by using *ppp* (*pianississimo*, sometimes called "triple piano") and *fff* (*fortississimo*, sometimes called "triple forte").

It's important to bear in mind that dynamic markings are not absolute. The symbol *mf* doesn't indicate an exact volume level—it just indicates that the music should be a little quieter than *f*, but louder than *mp*.

Changes in dynamic level can be either abrupt or gradual. Sudden changes are indicated by inserting a new dynamic marking in the music. (And if a strong, sudden accent is required, we can use a *sforzando* marking, abbreviated *sfz*.) Gradual increases and decreases in dynamic level are indicated by *crescendo* (or *cresc.*) and *decrescendo* (or *decresc.*) markings. *Diminuendo* (or *dim.*) can also be used to indicate a decrease in the dynamic level. "Hairpin" signs (<) (>) can also be used to indicate gradual changes, as in the following example:

Track 44
(0:43)

Note that in measures 1–4 of this example, the volume level abruptly alternates between *p* and *f*. Measure 5 starts at *mp*, before building gradually during the first "hairpin" to *ff*. The volume then gradually returns to *mp* during the second "hairpin."

Sometimes *ppp* or *fff* just isn't enough...

Some composers have used dynamic markings with more than three *f*'s or *p*'s:

- Tchaikovsky marked some *ffff* passages in his *1812 Overture*, and he wrote *pppppp* for a notorious bassoon solo in the first movement of the *Symphony No. 6*.

- Rachmaninoff used a *ffff* marking in his *Piano Prelude in C♯ Minor, Op. 3, No. 2*.

- Shostakovich wrote *ffff* and *fffff* in the first movement of his *Symphony No. 4*.

- Mahler needed a *fffff* marking in the second movement of his *Symphony No. 7*.

Gustav Mahler

Sometimes individual notes in a piece need to be played louder, without changing the dynamics of the other notes in that section. This is achieved by using either an *accent* mark (>), or (if the note needs to be very much louder) with a *marcato* mark (∧). These signs are used in the following example:

Track 44
(1:06)

In this example, the accents are used on all the downbeats except beat 4 of measure 2. The marcato markings are used to emphasize the strong accents during beat 4 of measure 2.

SLURS AND ARTICULATIONS

When musicians talk about *articulation*, they are referring to a performance technique that affects how single notes sound, and/or how the transition sounds between notes. Different articulations result in notes sounding long or short, connected or disconnected, and so on. Here is a summary of common articulations affecting the sound of individual notes (including some that we have seen before):

The first two articulations (the accent and marcato marks) cause the notes to be played louder. The third articulation is a *staccato*, indicating that the note sounds detached and separate from any surrounding notes. By contrast, the fourth articulation is a *tenuto*, indicating that the note should be held for its full duration.

Different instruments will achieve articulations through various physical playing techniques. For example, brass and woodwind instruments normally articulate by *tonguing* (using the tongue to control and break the airflow going into the instrument), whereas stringed instruments will use a mix of plucking and bowing.

If a musical phrase needs to be played smoothly and without separation (known as *legato* articulation), then a *slur* sign is used over the phrase. The following example shows this notation in the first measure, and also includes some staccato and tenuto markings in the subsequent measures:

Note the contrast between the first two measures: the same musical phrase is to be played legato (smooth and connected) in measure 1, and staccato (short and separated) in measure 2. The example then continues with some tenuto markings on the quarter notes in measure 3, leading to the final whole note.

For stringed instruments, legato phrasing normally requires the notes to be played in a single bow stroke (i.e., without moving the bow back and forth). In guitar music, the slur is best interpreted using a *hammer-on* (i.e., not plucking the string after the first note).

MORE TIME SIGNATURES

So far we've mostly been dealing with music in 4/4 time, which (as we saw back in Chapter 2) is the most commonly used time signature in Western music. Now it's time for us to learn some more time signatures. There are three overall categories of time signature that we need to be aware of: *simple*, *compound*, and *irregular* (also known as complex or asymmetric).

4/4 is an example of a *simple* time signature, in which the upper number indicates the number of beats in the measure, and the lower number indicates the note value representing one beat (we can call this the *beat unit*). In simple time signatures, each beat can be divided into two equal parts. The most common simple time signatures, in addition to 4/4, are 2/2, 2/4, and 3/4.

2/2 time has the same number of quarter notes per measure as 4/4, but the beat is felt differently: there are two half-note beats per measure.

 2/2 is also referred to as *cut time*, which has its own time signature symbol.

In the classical world, 2/2 time is often used for marches and fast orchestral music. In contemporary styles, the cut time signature is almost always used instead of 2/2 time, and is often found in Latin styles (especially samba). Here's a leadsheet excerpt from the tune "Morning Dance" by the Latin fusion group, Spyro Gyra, that uses cut time.

Morning Dance

By Jay Beckenstein

© 1979 Harlem Music, Inc. and Crosseyed Bear Music (BMI)
Administered by Harlem Music, Inc., 1762 Main Street, Buffalo, NY 14208
International Copyright Secured   All Rights Reserved

Notice that the tempo marking says "♩ = 100," indicating that the half note gets the beat (instead of the quarter note). This is very typical of samba charts: the measures zip by pretty quickly when you're reading!

On to 2/4 time, which simply has two quarter-note beats per measure.

Two measures of 2/4 have the same number of beats as one measure of 4/4. However, music written in 2/4 consists of two-beat measures, so each beat 1 is of equal importance. Here is an excerpt from Mozart's *Allegro in B♭ Major*, which uses the 2/4 time signature:

Allegro in B♭ Major, K. 3

By Wolfgang Amadeus Mozart

Next up is 3/4 or waltz time, which has three quarter-note beats per measure.

In addition to waltzes, this time signature is used for *minuets* and *scherzi* (often found as the third movements of symphonies). In contemporary music, 3/4 time is also found in some country ballads, as well as in traditional gospel styles.

Here's a piano arrangement of the immortal *Blue Danube Waltz*, written in 3/4 time:

Blue Danube Waltz

Music by Johann Strauss

Track 45
(0:05)

Now it's time to look at some *compound* time signatures, in which each main beat is divided into three equal parts. The top number of a compound time signature is normally a multiple of three, and if we divide this number by three we get the number of main beats (or pulses) per measure. For example, in 6/8 time, if we divide the top number by three, we get two main beats per measure. The bottom number of a compound time signature is normally eight (signifying eighth-note beats), but in fact the main pulse is felt on the *dotted quarter note* (i.e., every three eighth notes). So in 6/8 time, there are two main beats per measure, each lasting for a dotted quarter note (which is divided into three eighth notes). The most common compound time signatures are 6/8, 9/8, and 12/8.

6/8 time is found in some folk and traditional music, and in much classical music. 9/8 time is used in traditional gospel, as well as some classical music. 12/8 is found mainly in blues and R&B styles.

Next is a well-known example of a tune in 6/8, "House of the Rising Sun." Originally a Southern-American folk song, it was made famous by Eric Burdon and the Animals in their 1964 recording. This simple piano arrangement uses arpeggios in the left hand, and the melody in the right hand.

House of the Rising Sun

Southern American Folksong

Finally, we'll look at some *irregular* time signatures, in which the top number can be 5, 7, or a larger prime number. The bottom number of the irregular time signature will still represent the beat unit; for example, 5/4 time has five quarter-note beats per measure. Three of the more widely-known examples of 5/4 time are Paul Desmond's "Take Five" (from Dave Brubeck's pioneering jazz album *Time Out*), the theme from *Mission: Impossible*, and Jethro Tull's "Living in the Past." Other irregular time signatures include 7/4 (see Pink Floyd's "Money," included in our **Songs** section), as well as 7/8 and 11/8.

Here is the drum part for the intro to the Cream song "White Room." Although the main body of the tune is in 4/4 time, the intro is in 5/4.

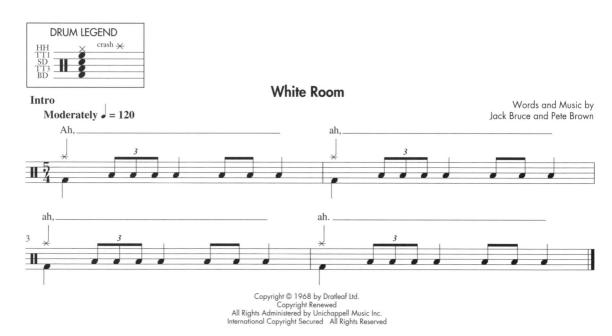

More Famous Songs with Irregular Time Signatures

Artist	Song	Tempo
Radiohead	"15 Step"	(5/4)
Gustav Holst	Mars: from *The Planets*	(5/4)
Sting	"Seven Days"	(5/4)
Peter Ilyich Tchaikovsky	Symphony No. 6 in B Minor: "Pathétique"	(movement II in 5/4)
The Beatles	"Happiness Is a Warm Gun"	(partially in 5/4)
George Harrison	"Within You, Without You"	(partially in 5/4)
Dave Brubeck	"Unsquare Dance"	(7/4)
Peter Gabriel	"Solsbury Hill"	(7/4)
Soundgarden	"Outshined"	(7/4)
Incubus	"Make Yourself"	(partially in 7/4)
Genesis	"Dance on a Volcano"	(7/8)
Devo	"Jocko Homo"	(partially in 7/8)
Grateful Dead	"The Eleven"	(11/8)
The Beatles	"Here Comes the Sun"	(mix of 7/8 and 11/8 in bridge)
Genesis	"Firth of Fifth"	(mix of 13/16 and 15/16 in intro)

Gustav Holst

MINOR SCALES AND KEYS

What's Ahead:

- Minor scales and key signatures
- Natural, melodic, and harmonic minor scales, and their diatonic triads
- The circle of 5ths/4ths applied to minor keys

MINOR SCALES AND KEY SIGNATURES

In this chapter we're going to learn about the various minor scales, and how they relate to minor keys and key signatures. Back in Chapter 3 we learned how to create all the major scales, and we saw that each major scale corresponded to a major key and used a major key signature. In other words, a song created from the C major scale would typically be in the key of C major, and would be written using the C major key signature (which, as you'll hopefully recall, has no sharps and no flats).

Well, I hate to break it to you, but all of those major key signatures we developed back in Chapter 3 also work for minor keys. If we reposition the C major scale to start on the note A (i.e., A–B–C–D–E–F–G–A), we get an A *natural minor scale* (equivalent to the A Aeolian mode that we saw in Chapter 6). This scale is used in the key of A minor, and the key signature again would have no sharps and no flats. The minor key that shares the same key signature as a major key is known as the *relative minor* of that major key. The relative minor always starts on the 6th degree of the corresponding major scale, as A is the 6th degree of the C major scale.

So if you see a key signature with no sharps and no flats, how do you know if you're in the key of C major or A minor? Well, you have to make a contextual judgment in the music: For example, if the "home base" (tonic) were C, you would most likely be in C major, whereas if the "home base" were A, you would be in A minor. Many tunes also move back and forth between the major and relative minor keys (for example, several Beatles songs, including "Yesterday").

Here's an updated version of the key signature summary from Chapter 3, now with all of the relative minor keys added.

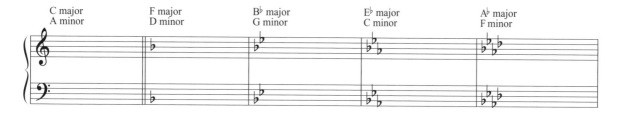

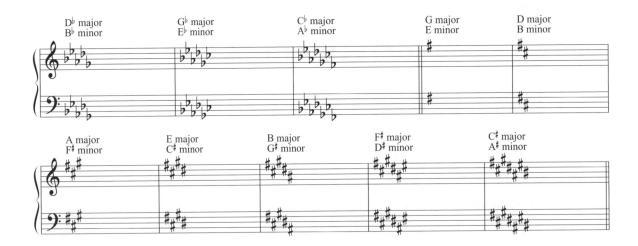

NATURAL, MELODIC, AND HARMONIC MINOR SCALES

So here's the other slightly tricky part: We can use more than one minor scale within a minor key. The natural minor scale will conform exactly to the minor key signature. For example, the A natural minor scale conforms exactly to the key signature of A minor (no sharps and no flats). In other words, no additional *accidentals* (sharps or flats) are needed if we are restricted to the A natural minor scale within the key of A minor. However, other minor scales *will* require us to contradict the minor key signature with accidentals.

> A lot of pop and rock music in minor keys just uses the natural minor scale, so for these tunes the extra sharps and flats are not needed. However, it is common in classical, jazz, Latin, and folk styles to mix the different minor scales within a minor key.

Now we'll investigate all three minor scales (natural, harmonic, and melodic). For consistency we'll start by building them all from middle C, and we'll see how they work within a minor-key context. We'll also build diatonic triads from each of these scales, and see how these triads are used (and mixed together) in some well-known pieces.

NATURAL MINOR SCALE

Here are two ways we can look at the C natural minor scale. On the left-hand side the scale is notated without the key signature of C minor, so we're using accidentals to create the specific sequence of whole steps and half steps needed (W = whole step; H = half step). On the right-hand side the scale is notated using the key signature of C minor, which has three flats (its relative major is E♭).

The natural minor scale (equivalent to the Aeolian mode) is widely used in contemporary styles. The first four intervals (whole–half–whole–whole) are shared by all of the minor scales, so the only differences are in the topmost intervals (in this case, half–whole–whole). Next up is the F natural minor scale, along with a famous movie theme based on that scale, notated with the key signature of F minor.

Track 46
(0:07)

Axel F
Theme from the Paramount Motion Picture BEVERLY HILLS COP

By Harold Faltermeyer

The key signature of four flats indicates that the tune is either in A♭ major or F minor. Notice that the tonic of this melody is F (rather than A♭): The melodic motifs start on F on beat 1 of each measure (or anticipating beat 1 in the case of measure 4). This means we are in the key of F minor. No additional sharps or flats are used, which means that the melody is contained within the F natural minor scale.

"Axel F" was the instrumental theme for the 1984 movie *Beverly Hills Cop*, composed and recorded by Harold Faltermeyer. Originally topping the US charts in the mid-1980s, the tune climbed the European charts two decades later as a remix by Crazy Frog. The title refers to Eddie Murphy's character (Axel Foley) in the movie.

Now we'll look at the triads that are diatonic to the natural minor scale. Chord progressions for many minor-key pop and rock songs employ only diatonic triads. The next example uses the B natural minor scale, and corresponding diatonic triads.

Track 46
(0:14)

Sting's "King of Pain" is in the key of B minor, and makes substantial use of the triads contained within the B natural minor scale, as shown in the following leadsheet excerpt.

King of Pain

Music and Lyrics by Sting

The B natural minor scale (or B Aeolian mode) is a repositioned or displaced version of the D major scale. Therefore the triads found in the B natural minor scale are the same as the diatonic triads in D major.

HARMONIC MINOR SCALE

We'll see two ways to look at the C *harmonic minor scale*. On the left-hand side we're using flats to create the sequence of whole steps and half steps, and on the right-hand side we're using the key signature of C minor.

Note the "3H" between the notes A♭ and B, signifying three half steps (or one-and-a-half steps). This unusually large interval contributes to the angular quality of this scale, which is characteristic of many ethnic and Middle Eastern melodies. We'll now have a look at the traditional Hebrew song "Havah Nagilah" (which you'll definitely need to learn if you ever get called for a Jewish wedding gig). This song uses the E harmonic minor scale:

Track 47
(0:07)

Havah Nagilah

Next we'll look at the triads that are diatonic to the harmonic minor scale. This scale still gives us a minor chord quality for I and IV, but a major quality for V. Here we have the D harmonic minor scale, and corresponding diatonic triads:

For comparison, here is the D natural minor scale, along with its diatonic triads:

We mentioned earlier that it is possible to use more than one minor scale within a minor key. This means that the melody and/or harmony may come from different minor scales as needed. The following excerpt from Handel's *Sarabande* is in the key of D minor, and contains melody notes and chords from both the D natural minor and D harmonic minor scales.

Sarabande in D Minor

By George Frideric Handel

We would not normally find chord symbols in classical music notation. However, the chord symbols are helpful here because they accurately reflect what is happening harmonically, and they enable us to see quickly which chords are being used from the diatonic triads within the minor scales.

The melody uses both the C from the D natural minor scale (in measure 5), and the C♯ from the D harmonic minor scale (in measure 8). The Dm and Gm chords belong to both the harmonic and natural minor scales; the A chords belong to the harmonic minor scale; and the F, C, and B♭maj7 (a larger version of B♭) chords belong to the natural minor scale. The C♯ melody note and the A major chord are also found in the D melodic minor scale (introduced in the next section); however, the use of the minor IV and major V chords in the same progression (Gm and A in this case) implies the harmonic minor scale.

MELODIC MINOR SCALE

Finally, we'll see two ways to look at the C *melodic minor scale*. Again, on the left-hand side we're using flats (actually just one flat this time) to create the sequence of whole and half steps, while on the right-hand side we're using the key signature of C minor.

Note the rather unusual sequence of four consecutive whole steps in this scale, from the 3rd up to the 7th degree. This minor scale is the most similar to the major scale. You only have to alter one note of the C major scale to get the C melodic minor scale: change E to E♭. The melodic minor scale is important in classical and jazz music, and in styles that make use of jazz harmony (i.e., the more advanced R&B and Latin styles).

We'll now have a look at an excerpt from a waltz by Edvard Grieg. This piece uses the A melodic minor scale:

Track 48
(0:07)

Waltz, Op. 38, No.7

By Edvard Grieg

Track 48
(0:14)

Note that the right-hand part consistently uses F# and G# within the key of A minor. This is like a "neon sign" advertising that the melodic minor scale is being used!

In some classical circles, the melodic minor scale is considered to have different ascending and descending forms: ascending as shown above, and descending the same as a natural minor scale. Different ascending and descending forms of this scale are never needed in contemporary applications.

Next we'll look at triads that are diatonic to the melodic minor scale. This scale now gives us major chords for IV and V, but still a minor quality for I. The next example shows the E melodic minor scale and corresponding diatonic triads:

Track 48
(0:34)

For comparison, here is the E natural minor scale, along with its diatonic triads:

Track 48
(0:55)

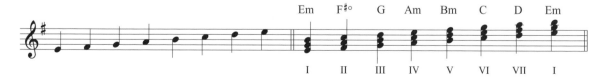

The popular English folk song "Scarborough Fair" is another example of a song that combines chords from different minor scales. This time we'll be using triads from both the E melodic minor and E natural minor scales. Look at the following piano arrangement, and note which chords are used to harmonize the melody.

Scarborough Fair

Traditional English

Track 48
(1:15)

Notice the left-hand Alberti-bass figures used in this piano arrangement. This is a common accompaniment device across a range of classical, pop, and folk styles.

The melody of this song uses both the C♯ from the E melodic minor scale (in measure 9), and the D from the E natural minor scale (in measures 7, 8, 12, and 14). (Alternatively, we could think of all the melody notes as coming from the E Dorian mode, which can also be used in a minor key.) The A major triads in measures 9 and 16 belong to the melodic minor scale, while all of the other chords are taken from the natural minor scale.

The folk song "Scarborough Fair" originated from a 17th-century Scottish ballad, and has since undergone numerous modifications and adaptations. The references to "Scarborough Fair" and "parsley, sage, rosemary, and thyme" occur in versions of the song from the 19th century onward. The most famous 20th-century version was recorded by Simon and Garfunkel in the 1960s, and was featured on the soundtrack to the movie *The Graduate*. The song also appears briefly in the 2003 Bill Murray movie, *Lost in Translation*.

Lastly, we'll look at another popular song that combines melody notes and chords from the different minor scales, in the key of E minor. The chords for "Greensleeves" are derived from the melodic and natural minor scales (as in the previous example), and the melody borrows from all the minor scales.

Greensleeves

16th Century Traditional English

At the beginning, the melody uses C (in measure 4) and D (in measure 6) from the natural minor scale. However, in measure 8 the D♯ appears, suggesting either harmonic or melodic minor. Then in measure 16 we have C♯ and D♯, both from melodic minor. In measures 20 and 28 we have C♯ and D, implying a mix of melodic and natural minor (or an E Dorian mode). All the chords originate from natural minor—except for the B major triads, which are from harmonic or melodic minor. Note the D/F♯ *passing chord* in measure 11: This is a D major chord placed over its third (F♯) in the bass. (These slash chords are treated more fully in Chapter 19.)

THE CIRCLE OF 5THS/4THS APPLIED TO MINOR KEYS

Back in Chapter 3, we showed all of the major scales and keys in a circle diagram (referred to as the *circle of keys*, or the *circle of 5ths/4ths*). Well, now we know that each key signature does double duty for both major and minor keys, so we can expand the original circle diagram to include all of the minor key signatures.

Each of the entries around the outside of the circle represent a major key (for example, halfway down on the right we have the key of A major, with three sharps in the key signature). Now for each major key, there is a corresponding relative minor key shown inside the circle (for example, halfway down on the right we have the key of F♯ minor, which shares its key signature with A major). To review: The relative minor is the 6th degree of the corresponding major key (i.e., F♯ is the 6th degree of A major).

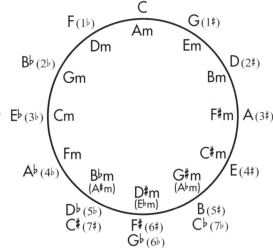

As with the major keys, we have an overlap zone at the bottom of the circle, where alternate (enharmonic) minor keys exist:

- B♭ minor (five flats) is equivalent to A♯ minor (seven sharps).
- D♯ minor (six sharps) is equivalent to E♭ minor (six flats).
- G♯ minor (five sharps) is equivalent to A♭ minor (seven flats).

When figuring out or recognizing minor key signatures, I recommend that you use the rules and methods we developed earlier for major keys, and then convert to the relative minor as the last stage in the process. The logic and concepts regarding the circle of 5ths and circle of 4ths will also apply to minor keys.

CHAPTER 10
MELODY HARMONIZATION AND COUNTERPOINT

> **What's Ahead:**
> - Different ways to enhance a melody
> - How to choose chords for a song
> - Counterpoint basics

DIFFERENT WAYS TO ENHANCE A MELODY

The most recognizable and memorable part of a song or classical piece is generally the melody. This is the part that people will sing or whistle, even if they don't know anything about music! However, as musicians, we are interested in different ways to support or enhance the melody by adding further notes and parts. We have already seen several leadsheet examples showing melodies with chord symbols, and in this chapter we'll be taking a closer look at how to add chords to an existing melody. We can also create one or more harmony lines below the main melody (often using 3rds and 6ths), which is a common way to generate background vocal and horn parts in contemporary styles. In general, adding harmony in this way will make the music sound bigger and fuller, and therefore more interesting to listen to.

Another way to enhance a melody is to add one or more independent melody lines, a technique known as *counterpoint*. This often occurs in classical music, as well as in more sophisticated jazz styles. In pop music, we find a technique called *harmonization by bass line*, which can be thought of as a type of counterpoint (although it does not adhere strictly to classical principles). And sometimes just a single note (often in the bass) is repeated against the melody; this is known as a *pedal point*, and it is found in both classical and contemporary styles. In general, we can say that adding chords or harmonies to a melody is mainly about the vertical combinations of notes, whereas creating counterpoint is mainly about the horizontal movement of individual parts. With these thoughts in mind, we'll take a simple tune in the key of C and demonstrate some ways in which the melody can be enhanced. First of all, here's our melody:

Now we'll apply a simple pedal point in the bass. Favorite choices for this are the tonic or the 5th degree of the key (C or G in this case). This example uses the tonic (C), repeated as whole notes:

Track 50
(0:11)

In this next stage, we're still using whole notes in the bass, but now with different pitches. This could imply the roots of a chord progression (in this case C–F–G–C), and/or it might be a slower-moving line (below the main melody) played in the bass. In this example we've added the implied chord symbols, even though the chords are not fully defined.

Track 50
(0:22)

Note that the melody notes on beat 1 of each measure are basic chord tones of the implied chord symbols: E is the third of C major, A is the third of F major, and D is the fifth of G major. The melody notes at the points of chord change are often basic chord tones in a simpler pop style.

Next we'll create some harmony parts to be used below the melody. For this we would normally stay within the key of the song (unless chords from other keys are being used—for more on this, see Chapter 18). Favorite intervals for these harmonies are 3rds and 6ths, due to their warm and consonant quality. The added parts should also work within the chord symbols, particularly on the strong beats (i.e., beats 1 and 3 of a 4/4 measure). Here's an example of 3rds added below the melody, a typical solution for vocal harmony lines:

Track 50
(0:34)

Note that the harmony notes on beat 1 of each measure are also basic chord tones: C is the root of C major, F is the root of F major, and B is the third of G major.

Here we have the same melody harmonized with 6ths:

Track 50
(0:45)

Note that the harmony notes on beat 1 of each measure are mostly basic chord tones: G is the fifth of C major, and C is the fifth of F major. The harmony note on beat 1 of measure 3 is F, which is the seventh of the implied G7 chord.

The next example harmonizes the melody with triads in the bass clef, again using the same C–F–G–C progression. Here we are using triad inversions to voice lead smoothly from left to right, a technique we first saw back in Chapter 5.

Track 50
(0:57)

We'll have more information soon on choosing the triads to harmonize a melody. But first let's add a counterpoint-type melody below the main melody, in the bass clef.

Track 50
(1:09)

A counterpoint line can have the same rhythm as the first melody, or (as in this case) it can have a different complementary rhythm. This is not "formal" counterpoint from a classical point of view, but it does demonstrate the addition of a separate melody line, as opposed to adding chords below a melody. We'll return to counterpoint at the end of this chapter.

HOW TO CHOOSE CHORDS FOR A SONG

If you've written a melody and would like to find the right chords to go with it, then this section should get you started. For now we're assuming that the melody is diatonic to a major key (hey, we have to start somewhere). Here we're going to introduce three main techniques to harmonize your melody:

- by primary triads;
- by diatonic triads and upper-structure triads;
- by bass line.

HARMONIZATION BY PRIMARY TRIADS

By *primary triads*, I mean the I, IV, and V triads in a major key (in the key of C major, these are the C major, F major, and G major triads). Many simpler pop, country, and folk songs are harmonized with primary triads.

This method involves looking at the melody and determining which notes from the primary triads are present. For this purpose, a melody note is more important if it occurs on a downbeat, especially on a *strong beat* (1 or 3 in 4/4 time). In general, longer notes would be more important than shorter notes when determining the harmony implications. Another factor to establish is the *chord rhythm* (how frequently the chords change). A reasonable starting point would be one chord per 4/4 measure; however (depending on the melody, style, and tempo), other chord rhythms such as two chords per measure (normally landing on beats 1 and 3), or one chord every two measures may be needed. These are good general points to bear in mind as we look at our first melody, the traditional song "Little Brown Jug."

Little Brown Jug

Words and Music by
Joseph E. Winner

For "Little Brown Jug" we will assume a one-chord-per-measure chord rhythm. To determine which of the primary triads (I, IV, or V) to use for each measure, we look at the melody to see which primary triad the melody is "closest to." In other words, if the melody uses some of the notes from a particular primary triad (often the case in simpler tunes), then that triad is likely to work for harmonization. In particular, the melody notes landing on beats 1 and 3 (in that order of importance) are the most significant. With this in mind, we'll look at each measure in the "Little Brown Jug" melody.

Measure 1: The melody notes on beats 1 and 3 are E and G, which are both within the I triad (C major). The note on the weak beats (2 and 4) is also G, so the C major triad is the best choice.

Measure 2: The melody notes on beats 1 and 3 are F and A, which are both within the IV triad (F major). The note on the weak beats (2 and 4) is also A, so the F major triad is the best choice.

Measure 3: The melody note on beats 1, 2, and 4 is B, which is found only in the V triad (G major), making this triad the best choice. The note on beat 3 is A, and while this is not a basic chord tone, it does not contradict the G chord (it temporarily creates a ninth on the chord).

Measure 4: The melody notes on beats 1 and 3 are C and E, which are both within the I triad (C major). The note on beat 2 is D, another temporary ninth, this time on the C major chord.

Note that the melody consists of four-measure phrases, and during the first phrase (measures 1–4) we start and end with the C major triad, which is the most restful chord available in the key of C major. This type of harmonization often occurs with simpler melodies, and gives us a clue about how to harmonize measures 5–8. The melody in measures 5–7 is substantially similar to measures 1–3, so we can use the C, F, and G major triads again to harmonize these measures.

Measure 8, however, seems less clear-cut, as the melody notes on beats 1 and 3 are D and C, which as a pair are not contained in any of the primary triads. However, we should, if possible, harmonize this measure with a C major chord, for symmetry with the first four-measure phrase and so that we can end on a restful chord. If we do this, the melody note on beat 1 (D) ends up being the ninth of the C chord, which then resolves to the root of the chord on beat 3. So all of this gives us the following harmonization:

Little Brown Jug

Track 51
(0:16)

extras

Note that the triads added in the bass clef are voice led from left to right. The first C triad is in first inversion, which leads to the F triad in root position and then to the G triad in second inversion, and so on. In this register, the triads don't get in the way of the melody, and yet are high enough to not sound "muddy" on the piano.

HARMONIZATION BY DIATONIC TRIADS AND UPPER-STRUCTURE TRIADS

You'll remember that we developed diatonic triads in various keys back in Chapter 5. Harmonizing by diatonic triads is the next step after harmonizing by primary triads. In the key of C, if we expanded our harmonization options to include all the diatonic triads (not just the primary triads of C, F, and G), we would have seven in total: C, Dm, Em, F, G, Am, B° (refer to **Track 25**). Our approach is similar to that taken in the last example: We look at the melody and determine if notes from the diatonic triads are being used. With this idea in mind, we'll examine an excerpt from the Eddie Holman pop hit "Hey There Lonely Girl (Hey There Lonely Boy)," to see how we might harmonize the melody with diatonic triads.

Hey There Lonely Girl (Hey There Lonely Boy)

Words and Music by
Earl Shuman and Leon Carr

This melody is suited to triad harmonization, as it uses arpeggios to outline various chords. We can analyze each measure of this melody as follows:

Measure 1: The melody notes E, C, and A together create an A minor triad, with the E falling on the strong beat (beat 1). A minor is the obvious chord choice.

Measure 2: The melody notes D, B, and G together create a G major triad, with the D falling on the strong beat (beat 1). G major is the obvious chord choice.

Measure 3: The melody notes C, A, and F together create an F major triad, with the C and A falling on the strong beats (beats 1 and 3). F major is the obvious chord choice.

Measure 4: The melody notes B and G are present in both the E minor and G major triads, with the B falling on the strong beat (beat 1). Both chords would be suitable choices. If it seems desirable to use a chord that has not been used yet (a subjective choice), then we choose E minor, as G major has already appeared in measure 2.

So all of this gives us the following harmonization of the melody:

Hey There Lonely Girl (Hey There Lonely Boy)

"But wait!" I hear you cry. "I know that tune, and our example doesn't quite sound like the record!" Well, I gotta admit... you're right! While this harmonization is perfectly okay, it isn't quite the same as the one on the record—because the record uses larger (four-part) chords instead of just triads. So we're now going to introduce harmonization by *upper-structure triads*, which is a neat way to find four-part (and larger) chords to fit your melodies. Using this concept, if we know that an A minor triad can be used to harmonize the first measure, then larger chords containing that A minor triad can also be used. One chord containing an A minor triad is the F major seventh four-part chord (which we first met on **Track 38**). We could say that A minor is an upper-structure triad of the F major seventh chord—it's built from the third of the chord, in fact. Similarly, the other triads that are used are also contained within larger four-part chords, as demonstrated in the following example:

Track 51
(0:33)

We can analyze this example as follows:

Measure 1: The A minor triad on beat 1 is contained within the F major seventh chord on beat 3. The A minor triad could therefore be termed an upper structure (built from the third) of the F major seventh chord.

Measure 2: The G major triad on beat 1 is contained within the E minor seventh chord on beat 3. The G major triad could therefore be termed an upper structure (built from the third) of the E minor seventh chord.

Measure 3: The F major triad on beat 1 is contained within the D minor seventh chord on beat 3. The F major triad could therefore be termed an upper structure (built from the third) of the D minor seventh chord.

Measure 4: The E minor triad on beat 1 is contained within the C major seventh chord on beat 3. The E minor triad could therefore be termed an upper structure (built from the third) of the C major seventh chord.

So instead of using the Am chord we could use Fmaj7; instead of using the G chord we could use Em7, etc. The next example shows these new bass notes below the previous triads, creating the four-part chords that we remember from the classic recording.

Hey There Lonely Girl (Hey There Lonely Boy)

Note that there are two lines of chord symbols shown. The bottom line contains the slash chord symbols, showing each upper-structure triad over its new bass note (for example, in measure 1 the Am triad has been placed over F in the bass). The top line shows the composite four-part chord symbols (for example, in measure 1 the Fmaj7 chord has been created by placing the Am chord over F in the bass).

Building triads from the third (to create four-part chords) is only one type of upper structure available. We can also build triads from the fifth, seventh, etc., to create or imply larger (five-part and six-part) chords. More later!

Comparing these two harmonizations of the song, we hear that the triads sound clean and simple, whereas the four-part chords sound more dense and full. Generally the size of the chords used (i.e., triads, four-part, five-part, etc.) is a stylistic choice. Subject to many variations and exceptions, we can say that the simpler contemporary styles (such as pop, rock, and country) are more likely to use triads, while more sophisticated styles (such as R&B, gospel, and especially jazz) will use larger chords.

In Chapter 19 we'll explore upper-structure voicings and slash chords in more detail!

HARMONIZATION BY BASS LINE

Harmonization by bass line involves composing a bass line underneath the melody, and then adding chords in between that work with both the melody and bass line. You can think of the bass line as a type of slow-moving counterpoint to the main melody. The bass line normally determines the chord rhythm. So if, for example, there were two different bass notes per measure, that would typically result in a two-chords-per-measure chord rhythm (very common in pop and rock styles). With rare exceptions, each note in the bass line needs to create a consonant interval (i.e., not dissonant or "clashing") with the melody at that point. In simpler contemporary styles, the majority of harmonization-by-bass-line situations occur in major keys, when the bass line is moving diatonically within the key. Next is one of the most famous melodies harmonized in this way, the theme from the 1960s gem "A Whiter Shade of Pale," by Procol Harum.

A Whiter Shade of Pale

Words and Music by
Keith Reid and Gary Brooker

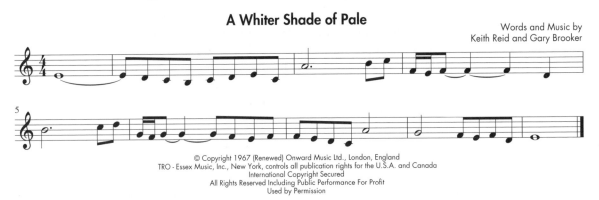

If you have a keyboard handy, go ahead and play this melody (preferably using an organ sound). Unless you've lived in a cave for the last few decades, you'll recognize it right away!

You'll notice that the melody is in the key of C, so our bass line would normally also be in the same key. When applying this technique, there are variables to consider, such as:

- How many bass notes to use per measure. For contemporary styles, one or two is the most common, with two being favored at slow-to-medium tempos.

- How the bass line should move (i.e., ascending vs. descending, large vs. small intervals, etc.). The majority of pop bass lines written this way descend in a scalewise pattern, mixing in some interval skips. At each stage you need to check the intervals created between the melody and bass line, especially on the strong beats of the measure. Some dissonance is okay on the weak beats, especially if the melody note is of shorter duration (i.e., an eighth or sixteenth note).

- What the starting note should be. A good default choice is the tonic of the key, which works in this case (C below E in the melody). Other diatonic notes are possible choices also. If you're using a scalewise bass line, you'll often need to look ahead and see what the implications of different starting notes are in later measures.

With these points in mind, let's start with the tonic (C) as the first bass note, and then descend scalewise within the C major scale (with some interval skips), using two bass notes per measure—just like they did on the record!

A Whiter Shade of Pale

Note that while most of this bass line descends by scalewise steps, there are some interval skips and variations:

- In measure 5, the bass moves up to G (instead of descending to B). This is a subjective decision based on the following considerations:
  - We can't continue descending forever; at some point we need to move up.
  - The note B would be in unison with the B in the melody, and while this would be okay, it doesn't sound as interesting as an interval created between two different notes. In this case the interval of G up to B creates a warm-sounding major 3rd (plus two octaves).
- In measure 7, the bass moves up to F (again instead of descending to B). This begins an ascending series of notes that takes us back to the starting note of C. Again, the choice of F here creates the consonant-sounding major 3rd, this time below the melody note A.

Note that the interval skips occurring in this bass line are 4ths and 5ths, which are considered very strong. These intervals are most commonly used for skips within a bass line that otherwise moves by scalewise intervals.

When trying to fit chords between a melody and a scalewise bass line, it will often be necessary to use a chord that is inverted over its third, fifth, or seventh in the bass, in order to stay diatonic to the key. This is another type of slash chord, as it is written with a slash in the chord symbol. For example, "C/G" means to place a C major triad over G (its fifth) in the bass.

So when choosing chords to fit between the melody and bass line, we'll not only be considering which triad is implied by the melody (as in the previous section of this chapter), but also we'll see if the bass note at that point has a useful relationship to the triad (i.e., is it the root, third, fifth, etc.). If the bass note is a chord tone other than the root, then this could imply a slash-chord harmonization.

With all these points in mind, let's now look at an arrangement of the organ intro for "A Whiter Shade of Pale." This shows the chord symbols fitted between the melody and bass line, and how these chords have been fleshed out in the right-hand part (including some counterpoint-type, secondary melody fragments).

A Whiter Shade of Pale

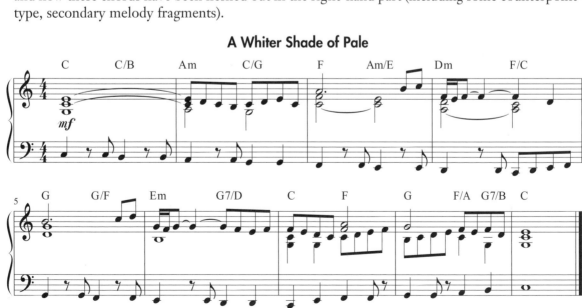

Let's take a closer look at the chord symbols and arranging choices in "A Whiter Shade of Pale":

Measure 1, beat 1: The C major triad (tonic chord of the key) is the logical diatonic chord choice, given the melody note of E and the C in the bass.

Measure 1, beat 3: The diatonic triad containing both the melody note (E) and the bass note (B) is E minor, so the slash chord Em/B would have been an option here. However, the composers went with the more tense-sounding C/B chord (i.e., continuing with the upper C triad, but now over B in the bass). This is dissonant due to the half step (plus two octaves) between the C (in the C major triad) and the B in the bass (implying a major seventh chord, placed over the seventh). This tension is an artistic judgment call and is generally okay, provided it resolves by the next chord (which it does here).

Measure 2, beat 1: The A minor triad is the logical diatonic chord choice, given the melody note of E and the A in the bass. Also, the melody note on beat 2 is C, which is the third of the chord.

Measure 2, beat 3: The melody note C on beat 3, together with the melody note E on beat 4 and the bass note G, all outline a C major chord inverted over its fifth (G) in the bass.

Measure 3, beat 1: The F major triad is the logical diatonic chord choice, given the melody note of A and the F in the bass.

Measure 3, beat 3: The diatonic triad containing both the melody note (A) and the bass note (E) is A minor, which placed over its fifth in the bass creates the slash chord Am/E. (Recall that in the similar circumstance of measure 1, the Em/B chord was an option.)

Measure 4, beat 1: The D minor triad is the logical diatonic chord choice, given the melody note of F (ornamented with the sixteenth-note E) and the D in the bass.

Measure 4, beat 3: The diatonic triad containing both the melody note F and the bass note C is F major, which placed over its fifth in the bass creates the slash chord F/C. In the bass, the eighth-note run (C–D–E–F) is used to connect to the G in the next measure.

Measure 5, beat 1: The G major triad is the logical diatonic chord choice, given the melody note of B and the bass note of G.

Measure 5, beat 3: The combination of B and F (melody and bass) is not present in a diatonic triad (except for the rarely used VII diminished), but is present in the G7 chord. The G/F here implies a dominant seventh chord inverted over its seventh, a chord that often moves to the next chord by a descending half step in the bass (as in this case). (See Chapter 12 for more about dominant-chord functionality.)

Measure 6, beat 1: The E minor triad is the logical diatonic chord choice, given the melody note of G (ornamented with the sixteenth-note F) and the E in the bass.

Measure 6, beat 3: The diatonic triad containing both the melody note G and the bass note D is G major, so the slash chord G/D would have been an option here. However, the composers went with the dominant chord G7/D to lead more strongly to the following C chord. The melody note F (the seventh of the G7 chord) appears twice during beats 3 and 4.

Measure 7, beat 1: Here the harmony feels like it should move back to the tonic chord, given the preceding dominant chord. Although the melody note on beat 1 is F, it quickly resolves to E (the third of the C chord) on the next eighth note. So with the C in the bass, this implies a Csus4 chord lasting for half a beat, before resolving to the C chord. In practice we just show the C chord symbol for two beats, with the understanding that this chord is suspended for the short duration of the F in the melody. Also, in this arrangement the bass moves to E (briefly implying a C/E chord) on beat 2.

Measure 7, beat 3: The F major triad is the logical diatonic chord choice, given the melody note of A and the F in the bass. A counterpoint line of C–D–E–F, in eighth notes, has also been added to support the main melody.

Measure 8, beat 1: The default assumption here is a G major chord, given the G in both the melody and bass. Also, the G (V) chord is useful here to lead back to the tonic (I) chord in the next section. Although there is a unison between the melody and bass, it is made more interesting by the eighth-note counterpoint line (B–C–D–E) under the main melody.

Measure 8, beat 3: The diatonic triads containing both the melody note F and the bass note A are F major and D minor. In this situation, where the bass line is ascending, the major chord (inverted over its third) sounds stronger than the minor chord (inverted over its fifth), so we go with the F/A slash chord.

Measure 8, beat 4: There is an extra bass note (B) here to lead back to the C at the start of the next section. This suggests a busier chord rhythm, with chords falling on beats 3 and 4 in this measure. As in measure 5, the combination of B and F most often suggests a G7 dominant chord. This time, with B in the bass, the resulting slash chord symbol is G7/B.

Procol Harum's "A Whiter Shade of Pale" has become one of the most enduring rock songs of all time, not least because of Matthew Fisher's classically-influenced organ part on the recording. Originally released in 1967, it topped the charts in several countries and went on to become the most-played record ever in the UK (according to a 2004 survey). The song has since been covered by hundreds of artists, including Eric Clapton, Joe Cocker, Willie Nelson, and Michael Bolton.

Photo by Gered Mankowitz/Redferns
Procol Harum

COUNTERPOINT BASICS

As mentioned at the outset of this chapter, *counterpoint* is the use of two (or more) separate melody lines played simultaneously. Classical counterpoint melodies (for example, the left- and right-hand piano parts in a Bach two-part invention) will generally have the following characteristics:

- Both lines will be of equal melodic importance (i.e., one line should not be subsidiary to the other).
- Each melodic line should make sense and stand on its own.
- The two melodic lines must fit together in a way that implies the harmonic structure of the piece.
- The intervals created between the melodic lines will usually be consonant. Any dissonant intervals used will normally be resolved afterwards.

For our first counterpoint example, we'll start with a well-known melody to which we will fit a counterpoint line. Here's an excerpt from the traditional song "Abide with Me":

Abide with Me

To add a simple counterpoint, we'll compose a line with rhythms identical to those of the first melody (this is sometimes referred to as a 1:1 rhythmic ratio). Also, we'll emphasize consonant intervals between the melodies (such as 3rds and 6ths) and avoid melodic intervals larger than a 6th in the counterpoint line, as shown in the following example:

Abide with Me

Track 52
(0:15)

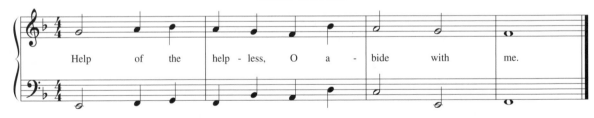

Now it's time to take a closer look at this counterpoint line and the intervals it creates with the first melody. As the line is written in the bass clef, we can also consider the harmonic implications (i.e., chord symbols) of the counterpoint line.

Measure 1: Here the line moves in scalewise steps below the first melody, resulting in 3rds (plus two octaves) between the two lines. The harmonic implication is a C/E chord on beat 1, and an F chord on beat 3.

Measure 2: Here the line uses two ascending 4ths, separated by a descending 2nd. After beat 1, this results in 6ths (plus one octave) between the two lines. The harmonic implication is an F chord on beat 1, and an F/A chord on beat 3.

Measure 3: Here the line uses a descending 6th, which is normally the largest interval that would be used in this type of counterpoint. Note the smaller 2nds before and after this larger interval, which help us to "digest" this larger interval. This results in a 6th (plus one octave) and a 3rd (plus two octaves) between the two lines. The harmonic implication is an F/C chord on beat 1, and a C/E chord on beat 3.

Measure 4: In the last measure, the counterpoint line is in unison with the first melody (implying an F chord). This typically occurs at the end of a piece.

Our next counterpoint example features contrasting rhythms between the two melodies (i.e., no longer a 1:1 rhythmic ratio). This is an excerpt from *Invention No. 13 in A Minor* by J.S. Bach, the most famous classical composer to use counterpoint techniques. This example uses *rhythmic displacement*, which is typical of more sophisticated counterpoint. For example, in measure 1 in the treble clef, we have two beats of sixteenth notes followed by two beats of eighth notes, and this rhythmic pattern is then repeated (or displaced) two beats later in the bass clef.

Invention No. 13

By Johann Sebastian Bach

Track 52
(0:30)

Note the elegant way the two melodic lines fit together, and that each melody makes sense and sounds musical on its own. Also, a lot of consonant intervals (3rds and 6ths, plus one or two octaves) are created vertically between the two melodic lines. Now we'll take a closer look at this example, including the harmonic implications.

Measure 1: In the treble clef, during beat 1 the notes collectively form an A minor triad, and during beat 2 the notes collectively (together with the G♯ in the bass clef) form an E7 dominant chord. This harmonic implication (Am–E7) is then repeated during beats 3–4. As with all the measures in this example, sixteenth notes are used in the right hand on beats 1–2 and in the left hand on beats 3–4, while eighth notes are used in the right hand on beats 3–4 and in the left hand on beats 1–2: Examples of rhythmic displacement.

Measure 2: As in measure 1, the harmonic implication is Am (beats 1 and 3) and E7 (beats 2 and 4). This time the right hand rests on beat 4, which ends the melodic phrase.

Measure 3: Between both parts during beats 1–2, the notes collectively form an A minor triad (with the brief implication of an Am7 chord, due to the G in the treble clef on the last sixteenth note of beat 2). Then between both parts during beats 3–4, the notes collectively form a D minor triad (with the brief implication of a Dm7 chord, due to the C in the bass clef on the last sixteenth note of beat 4).

Measure 4: Between both parts during beats 1–2, the notes collectively form a G7 dominant chord, and because the note B occurs in the lower part of the bass clef on beat 1, we could say that a G7/B chord is implied. Then between both parts during beats 3–4, the notes collectively form a C major triad (with the brief implication of a Cmaj7 chord, due to the B in the bass clef on the last sixteenth note of beat 4).

try this

You too can write your own counterpoint melodies! Start off with a simple four- or eight-measure melodic phrase, with rhythmic values no smaller than eighth notes (at least for now). Make sure that the last melody note (probably falling on beat 1 or beat 3 of the last measure) is the tonic of the key. Then create a counterpoint line to the first melody, using the same rhythms (i.e., a 1:1 rhythmic ratio, as in "Abide with Me"). Also, make sure to use consonant intervals (especially 3rds and 6ths) between the counterpoint and the first melody line, and finish on the tonic of the key below the last note in the first melody (creating a unison interval). When you have written a few of these simpler counterpoint examples, you can move on to some pieces using different rhythmic relationships between the melodies. Oh, and don't forget to listen to some Bach stuff. His inventions, chorales, and fugues are a good place to start. Counterpoint doesn't get any better than that!

Counterpoint Isn't Just for Classical Music

Although counterpoint was made famous by the Baroque composer Johann Sebastian Bach, this compositional technique is also used in various pop, jazz, and musical theater styles.

- In the progressive rock era of the early 1970s, bands such as Yes, Gentle Giant, and Gryphon made significant use of counterpoint.

- Notable usages of counterpoint in jazz include works by Stan Getz, Gerry Mulligan, Bill Holman, and the improvisations of pianist Denny Zeitlin.

- In the world of musical theater, songs from *Sweeney Todd* (Stephen Sondheim), *Les Misérables* (Claude-Michel Schönberg), and *La Cage aux Folles* (Jerry Herman) feature various types of counterpoint.

Photo provided by Photofest
Stephen Sondheim

Intermediate Stuff

SECTION

3

CHAPTER 11
FIVE-PART CHORDS

What's Ahead:
- Creating five-part chords
- Five-part chord alterations
- Major and minor add9 chords

CREATING FIVE-PART CHORDS

Following on from the four-part chords explained in Chapter 7, we're now going to derive some *five-part chords* (i.e., chords containing five notes). Most five-part chords are ninth chords, with the fifth note of the chord being the interval of a 9th above the root. The most common five-part chords used in pop and jazz styles are the *major ninth, major 6/9, minor ninth, minor/major ninth, minor 6/9, dominant ninth,* and *suspended dominant ninth* chords. Again, we will build each chord up from the root, using specific intervals as follows:

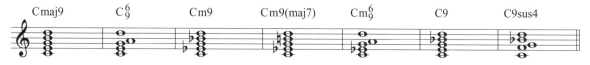

These chords are formed by building the following intervals above the root:

- major ninth chord: major 3rd, perfect 5th, major 7th, major 9th
- major 6/9 chord: major 3rd, perfect 5th, major 6th, major 9th
- minor ninth chord: minor 3rd, perfect 5th, minor 7th, major 9th
- minor/major ninth chord: minor 3rd, perfect 5th, major 7th, major 9th
- minor 6/9 chord: minor 3rd, perfect 5th, major 6th, major 9th
- dominant ninth chord: major 3rd, perfect 5th, minor 7th, major 9th
- suspended dominant ninth chord: perfect 4th, perfect 5th, minor 7th, major 9th

As with the four-part chord symbols we saw in Chapter 7, some of these five-part chord symbols have just a letter name and one or more numbers (i.e., "C_9^6" and "C9"). In this case, if the first number is less than "7" (as in "C_9^6"), the chord has a major quality; otherwise the chord has a dominant quality. Again, be careful to distinguish between interval descriptions and chord descriptions: For example, the minor ninth chord contains the interval of a major 9th from the root up to the ninth.

Some other points to be aware of regarding these chords:

- The chord symbol "Cm9(maj7)" has a suffix that refers to both minor and major, similar to the "Cm(maj7)" symbol we saw in Chapter 7. The minor part ("m") refers to the interval of a minor 3rd from the root up to the third, and the major part ("maj") refers to the interval of a major 7th from the root up to the seventh.
- The suspended dominant ninth chord (C9sus4) is a dominant ninth chord in which the third (E) has been replaced by the fourth (F); it's similar to the suspended dominant seventh chord we saw back in Chapter 7.

You'll notice that each chord on **Track 53** (first section) contains an interval of a major 9th from the root up to the ninth. All ninth chords will contain the note that is a major 9th above the root, with the exception of some altered dominant chords that we'll see later in this chapter. While it is technically possible to alter the ninth (i.e., add a minor or augmented 9th) of a non-dominant chord, the results will not be useful, at least for the vast majority of Western music styles. So... I recommend that you don't do this on any music that you're getting paid for!

Now it's time for another general rule about chords: The larger the chord is (i.e., the more notes it has), the less likely it is to be played as a simple vertical stack of pitches. This applies especially to five-part (and larger) chords. For example, let's say we saw a "Cmaj9" chord symbol in a song and we played it as in the example on **Track 53**. Well, although this would be technically correct, it would not sound especially interesting or stylistic. So we need to get beyond just the simple spelling of the chord (important as that is), and get to know how the chord might be voiced in a real-world situation.

In the last chapter, we were introduced to some upper-structure triad voicings for four-part chords used to harmonize a melody. Upper structures are also very useful for voicing five-part chords in contemporary styles. For instance, one can build an upper four-part chord from the third or fifth of the original five-part chord. Let's hear this principle at work on some five-part chords in the key of E♭ major:

In each measure above, the first chord is a five-part chord (except in measure 3) and the second chord is an upper structure, which when placed over the root of the first chord creates the chord quality needed. So why do we have a Gm7 (instead of a five-part Gm9) at the start of measure 3? Well, we're about to use these chords in a song in the key of E♭, and while we could build a minor ninth chord from G (which is the 3rd scale degree of the key), the ninth of this chord would be the note A, which is not contained within the key of E♭. This would not be a problem in jazzier or more sophisticated styles, but will most likely be an issue in more commercial situations. So to avoid this problem we just have a four-part Gm7 chord in measure 3, with its upper-structure B♭ major triad.

We can comment further on each chord and its upper structure as follows:

Measure 1:   The Gm7 is an upper structure built from the third of E♭maj9.

Measure 2:   The A♭maj7 is an upper structure built from the third of Fm9.

Measure 3:	The B♭ triad is an upper structure built from the third of Gm7.
Measure 4:	The Cm7 is an upper structure built from the third of A♭maj9.
Measure 5:	The Fm7 is an upper structure built from the fifth of B♭9sus4.

All of the upper structures are shown in root position—except for the last chord, where the F minor seventh chord (upper structure from the B♭ suspended dominant ninth chord) is in third inversion. When applying these upper-structure voicings to a song, we can invert and voice lead them as necessary to ensure smooth movement between chords.

Next we're going to look at an excerpt from the '70s pop ballad "Make It with You," by Bread. This is in the key of E♭ and uses the five-part chord symbols shown in the previous example.

Make It with You

Words and Music by
David Gates

Now we're going to create a simple piano *comping* (or accompaniment) part for this song using upper-structure voicings to interpret the chord symbols.

Track 53
(0:46)

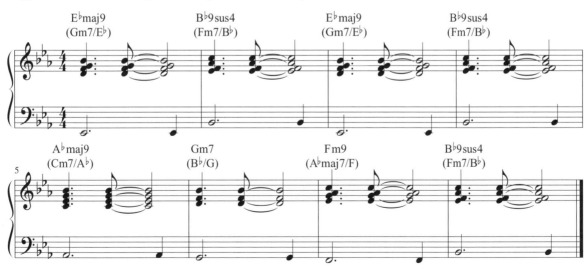

Note that there are two lines of chord symbols in "Make It with You." The bottom line contains the slash chord symbols, showing each upper structure over its new bass note (for example, in measure 1 the Gm7 chord has been placed over E♭ in the bass). The top line shows the composite chord symbols (for example, in measure 1 the E♭maj9 chord has been created by placing the Gm7 chord over E♭ in the bass). Note the inversions used in the treble-clef part: The upper Gm7 in measure 1 is in second inversion, leading to the upper Fm7 in measure 2 in third inversion, and so on.

Check all of the previous chords and voicings against **Track 53** (section starting 0:19) to see how each composite symbol has been voiced using the appropriate upper structure.

FIVE-PART CHORD ALTERATIONS

An *altered* five-part chord is a chord in which the fifth and/or ninth have/has been raised or lowered by a half step. In Chapter 7 we saw that altered four-part chords had the fifth either sharped or flatted (leaving the definitive third and seventh of the chord intact) and we noted that we could alter the fifth on major seventh, minor seventh, and dominant seventh chords (as on **Track 42**). Similarly, we can alter the fifth (without altering the ninth) on major ninth, minor ninth, and dominant ninth chords. However, only three types of ninth chords with altered fifths are in common usage: The minor ninth with flatted fifth and the dominant ninth with either flatted or sharped fifth.

As mentioned earlier, the only time we will alter the ninth within a chord (at least in conventional Western harmony) is on dominant chords. The altered ninth can be the only alteration, or it can be combined with an altered fifth.

The following example, showing five-part altered chords, is divided into three parts: The first part is for five-part chords with an altered fifth only (as mentioned above, only three of these chords are in common usage). The second part is for five-part chords with an altered ninth; these will only be dominant chords. The third part is for five-part chords with an altered fifth and altered ninth; again, these will only be dominant chords.

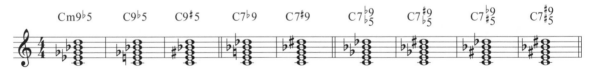

These five-part altered chords can be summarized as follows:

PART 1 (five-part chords with altered fifth)
- minor ninth chords: In measure 1, the fifth is lowered by a half step to G♭, creating the Cm9♭5 chord.
- dominant ninth chords: In measure 2, the fifth is lowered by a half step to G♭, creating the C9♭5 chord.

  In measure 3, the fifth is raised by a half step to G♯, creating the C9♯5 chord.

PART 2 (five-part chords with altered ninth)
- dominant chords: In measure 4, the ninth is lowered by a half step to D♭, creating the C7♭9 chord.

  In measure 5, the ninth is raised by a half step to D♯, creating the C7♯9 chord.

PART 3 (five-part chords with altered fifth and altered ninth)

- dominant chords: In measure 6, the fifth is lowered by a half step to G♭, and the ninth is lowered by half step to D♭, creating the C7♭9♭5 chord.

  In measure 7, the fifth is lowered by a half step to G♭, and the ninth is raised by half step to D♯, creating the C7♯9♭5 chord.

  In measure 8, the fifth is raised by a half step to G♯, and the ninth is lowered by half step to D♭, creating the C7♭9♯5 chord.

  In measure 9, the fifth is raised by a half step to G♯, and the ninth is raised by half step to D♯, creating the C7♯9♯5 chord.

Some other points to be aware of regarding these five-part altered chords:

- Although all combinations of altered fifths and ninths on the dominant chord (measures 6–9) are available, in practice the combination of a flatted fifth and sharped ninth (as in C7♯9♭5) is used less frequently than the other combinations.

- On altered chords, the flatted fifth ("♭5") is sometimes written as a sharped eleventh ("♯11"), and the sharped fifth ("♯5") is sometimes written as a flatted thirteenth ("♭13"). These terms are considered interchangeable within chord symbols. (See Chapter 16 for more information on larger chords with elevenths and thirteenths.)

- Sometimes you will see the chord-symbol suffix "7alt" (as in the chord symbol "C7alt"). This means that all altered fifths and ninths are available to use at the player's discretion. In many cases a good response to this symbol is to use a dominant seventh with sharped ninth and sharped fifth chord (i.e., "C7alt" is interpreted as C7♯9♯5), unless another combination of alterations is suggested by the musical context.

- Most of the altered dominant chords shown here are commonly used in jazz and in the jazzier pop/R&B styles—except for the dominant ninth with altered fifth (measures 2–3) which is more prevalent in Broadway and show tunes. This chord also implies a *whole-tone scale* (more about this in Chapter 17).

We saw earlier in this chapter that larger chords are not normally voiced in the same way as their stacks are literally spelled. Instead, upper-structure voicings are often used to apply these chords in real-world contexts. Well, this is also true of five-part altered chords. With this in mind, our next excerpt is from the Leon Russell classic "This Masquerade" (recorded by George Benson, among others). We'll look at the chords and upper-structure voicings used for an eight-measure section of the verse. The original chord symbols are a mix of triads, four-part and five-part chords, including some altered dominant chords. First of all we'll investigate the upper structures available on some of these chords.

Track 54
(0:27)

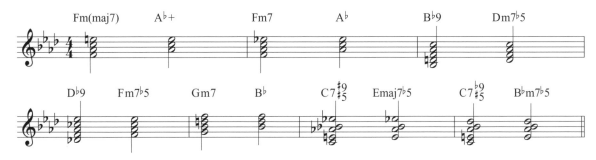

In each measure on the previous page, the first chord is a literal spelling of the symbol used in the song (either a four- or five-part chord), and the second chord is an upper structure which, when placed over the root of the first chord, creates the chord quality needed. We can comment on each chord and upper structure as follows:

Measure 1: The A♭ augmented triad is an upper structure built from the third of the Fm(maj7) chord (refer to **Track 37**, measure 6).

Measure 2: The A♭ major triad is an upper structure built from the third of the Fm7 chord (refer to **Track 53**, section starting 0:19, measure 6).

Measure 3: The Dm7♭5 chord is an upper structure built from the third of the B♭9 chord (refer to **Track 53**, first section, measure 6).

Measure 4: The Fm7♭5 chord is an upper structure built from the third of the D♭9 chord (refer to **Track 53**, first section, measure 6).

Measure 5: The B♭ major triad is an upper structure built from the third of the Gm7 chord (refer to **Track 53**, section starting 0:19, measure 3).

Measure 6: The Emaj7♭5 chord (refer to **Track 42**, measure 2) is an upper structure built from the third of the C7$^{\sharp9}_{\sharp5}$ chord (refer to **Track 54**, first section, measure 9). The top note is shown as E♭, rather than D♯, for consistency with the song's key signature of A♭ major.

Measure 7: The B♭m7♭5 chord is an upper structure built from the seventh of the C7$^{\flat9}_{\sharp5}$ chord (refer to **Track 54**, first section, measure 8). This particular upper structure is used in second inversion (whereas all the others are in root position).

Next we have the leadsheet from "This Masquerade," which includes the chord symbols from the previous example.

This Masquerade

Words and Music by
Leon Russell

Are we real-ly hap - py here ___ with this lone - ly game we play, ___

look - ing for words ___ to say? ___

Now we're going to create a piano comping part for this song (in a simple Latin/pop style) using upper-structure voicings to interpret the chord symbols.

Track 54
(1:02)

nuts
& bolts

Again there are two lines of chord symbols showing both the composite and the slash chord symbols. The first chord is simply an F minor triad, so we have shown the slash chord symbol "Fm/F" to indicate that the F minor triad has been placed over its root. All of the other chord symbols are four- or five-part, and for these, either triad or four-part upper structures have been used. For example:

- In measure 2 the A♭ augmented triad has been placed over F in the bass, creating the Fm(maj7) chord.
- In measure 8 the Emaj7♭5 chord has been placed over C in the bass, creating the C7$^{\sharp9}_{\sharp5}$ chord.

Again, note the inversions used in the treble-clef part: For example, the upper B♭m7♭5 at the end of measure 8 is in second inversion to voice lead smoothly from the upper Emaj7♭5 in root position.

try this

Check the above chords and voicings against those on **Track 54** (section starting 0:27) to see how each composite symbol has been voiced using the appropriate upper structure.

MAJOR AND MINOR ADD9 CHORDS

A major or minor *add9 chord* is the result of adding a ninth to a major or minor triad. This is equivalent to a major or minor ninth chord (refer to **Track 53**, measures 1 and 3), but with the seventh omitted. Here are examples of major and minor add9 chords:

audio
tracks
55

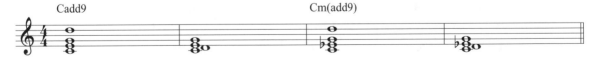

There are two basic configurations shown for these add9 chords. In measures 1 and 3 the ninth is shown as a major 9th above the root, and in measures 2 and 4 the ninth is shown as a major 2nd above the root. Functionally the note D is really a ninth on these chords, even if it is voiced just above the root (although you may sometimes see the more colloquial chord symbol "Cadd2" used in this situation). Another variation on the add9 chord is to omit the third—sometimes written as "Cadd9(omit 3rd)" or "Cadd9(no3rd)." This is equivalent to the Csus2 chord we heard on **Track 29**.

These add9 chords are commonly used in pop styles, especially ballads. Here's a leadsheeet excerpt from the James Ingram ballad "Just Once," which uses add9 chords together with some other four- and five-part chords.

Just Once

Again we'll create a piano comping part (this time in a pop ballad style) using a mix of add9 chords and upper-structure voicings to interpret the chord symbols.

We can comment on the voicings used as follows:

- Add9 chords with the ninth placed next to the root have been used for the Cadd9 and Am(add9) chords in measures 1 and 4.
- Four-part upper structures have been used on the Fmaj9 (building an Am7 from the third) and Am9 (building a Cmaj7 from the third) in measures 1 and 2.
- Triad upper structures have been used on the Em7 (building a G triad from the third) and Dm7 (building an F triad from the third) in measures 2, 3, and 4.
- The G/F in measure 3 is a slash chord: a G7 inverted over its seventh in the bass.

This mix of add9 chords and triad/four-part upper structures is a typical contemporary sound.

CHAPTER 12
THE II–V–I PROGRESSION

What's Ahead:

- Diatonic solfege and resolutions in major keys
- The II–V–I progression in major keys
- Chromatic solfege and resolutions in minor keys
- The II–V–I progression in minor keys
- Combining II–V–I progressions from major and minor keys

DIATONIC SOLFEGE AND RESOLUTIONS IN MAJOR KEYS

Solfege is a system of syllables we can use to label the pitches in a major scale. One famous solfege user was Julie Andrews in *The Sound of Music.* You may have encountered solfege syllables if you have studied ear training or sightsinging. Although these syllables are really just labeling tools, they help us understand the resolutions that occur within a scale or key. Here is a C major scale shown with solfege syllables assigned to each pitch within the scale:

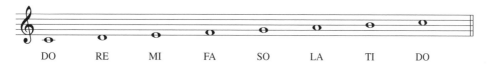

| DO | RE | MI | FA | SO | LA | TI | DO |

The solfege system was first introduced by Guido of Arezzo, Italy, during the early part of the 11th century. He noticed that each line of the hymn *Ut queant laxis* began on a different degree of the scale. This prompted him to assign the first syllable of each Latin phrase used in the hymn to each scale degree in succession.

What we will see is that each of these scale degrees has a unique active or resting property with respect to the tonic of the key (or DO). These properties are fundamental to understanding how melodies and chord progressions work in many Western music styles. The solfege syllables work in all keys using a movable DO system; in other words, DO can be assigned to the tonic of any key and the active and resting properties will work in exactly the same way. Every major scale degree has these properties:

DO: This is the tonic or "home base" of the major key we are using, and so this scale degree is the most restful or "resolved" within the major scale.

RE: This is an active tone that generally wants to resolve down by a whole step to DO (or up to MI).

MI: This is a resting tone within the major scale; it is very definitive, as it clearly signifies a major-key quality.

FA: This is an active tone that normally wants to resolve down by a half step to MI. Because the half step is very strong and "leading," FA is a very active tone within the key.

SO: This is another resting tone within the major scale; SO has a very stable quality. SO is also written as SOL in more formal/classical circles.

LA: This is an active tone that generally wants to resolve down by a whole step to SO (or up to DO via TI).

TI: This is another active tone which normally wants to resolve up to DO by half step.

These properties can be summarized as follows:

- DO, MI, and SO are the resting or "resolved" tones of the major scale.
- RE and LA are mildly active, as they resolve to adjacent resting tones by a whole step.
- FA and TI are very active, as they resolve to adjacent resting tones by a half step.

We can therefore say that the main active-to-resting resolutions within a major key are:

- RE down to DO (by whole step);
- FA down to MI (by half step);
- LA down to SO (by whole step);
- TI up to DO (by half step).

Listen for these resolutions on **Track 56**:

THE II–V–I PROGRESSION IN MAJOR KEYS

A *II–V–I progression* is a series of chords built from the 2nd, 5th, and 1st degrees of the key. Back in Chapter 7 we derived the four-part chords that were diatonic to the key of C major (refer to **Track 38**). If we simply extract the chords built on the 2nd, 5th, and 1st scale degrees from this series of four-part chords, we get the following (notice that there are two forms of I chord shown; these are often used interchangeably in jazz):

Track 56
(0:19)

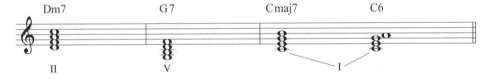

It turns out that, when using four-part (or larger) chords, this progression is uniquely good at defining the key to our ear, as it provides the critical active-to-resting resolutions (FA–MI and TI–DO) within the key. This is significant in jazz and jazz-influenced styles in which the music often moves through different momentary keys during the course of a tune. The definition provided by these resolutions helps us keep track of where the tune is going—a very good thing for all you aspiring jazz musicians out there!

Track 56
(0:32)

In Chapter 7 we saw that it was the third and seventh of each four-part chord that helps define the chord quality (i.e., major seventh, minor seventh, etc.) to our ear. Let's now take another look at this II–V–I progression in C major (using the major seventh form of the I chord) just isolating the thirds and sevenths of the chords in the treble clef (what I call a "7–3" *voicing*), with the root of each chord in the bass clef.

We can make the following observations about this II–V–I progression in major:

- The third and seventh of each chord completely define the minor seventh, dominant seventh, and major seventh chord qualities (refer to Chapter 7 and Track 37).

- This progression enables us to move between DO and TI of the key (from the IIm7 chord to the V7 chord) and between FA and MI of the key (from the V7 chord to the Imaj7 chord). Both of the leading half steps in the major scale are used, which is the most efficient way to let our ear know which key we are in.

- The root movement of the II–V–I progression (D–G–C in this case) uses a strong and leading circle-of-fifths motion (see Chapter 3).

Jazz tunes make frequent use of II–V–I progressions and partial II–V–I progressions (for example, the II–V, the V–I, or just the V chord). This can occur within the key signature of the song, and also within different momentary keys used in the harmony. In this chapter we'll begin to see these concepts at work in some classic jazz tunes. In Chapter 18 we'll explore the concept of momentary keys in more detail.

Our first song example in this chapter is the jazz standard "Misty," which uses II–V–I harmony in major keys. Here's a leadsheet for the verse of this song:

Misty

Words by Johnny Burke
Music by Erroll Garner

We can summarize the complete and partial II–V–I progressions in "Misty."

Complete: B♭m7–E♭7–A♭maj7 (measures 2–3) is a II–V–I in the momentary key of A♭.

Partial (II–V):   A♭m7–D♭7 (measure 4) is a II–V in the momentary key of G♭.
                 Fm7–B♭7 (measure 6) is a II–V in the overall key of the song (E♭).

Partial (V only): The G7, C7, and F7 chords (measures 7 and 8) are V chords in the momentary keys of C, F, and B♭, respectively.
                 The B♭7 chord in measure 8 is a V chord in the overall key of the song (E♭).

In addition to the II–V–I chords in major, "Misty" has a substitute chord: The Cm7 chord in measure 5 can be considered a substitute for an E♭maj7 chord (a *VI-for-I substitution* in the key of E♭ major). This is based on the principle that the II–V–I chords are definitive chords within a key (once the harmony gets to four-part chords or above) and that other available chords can be understood as substitutes for these definitive chords. We'll discuss these substitute relationships more fully in Chapter 13.

There are two different ways that we can use solfege when working with this type of song, which can be termed *moveable DO* and *fixed DO*.

- Using the former, we move DO around to the tonic of each momentary key. For example, we start out with E♭ as DO because we are in the key of E♭. Then we reassign DO to A♭ in measures 2–3, as we have changed to the momentary key of A♭, and so on.

- Using the latter, we keep DO assigned to the tonic of the tune (E♭ in this case) throughout. We then use chromatic solfege syllables (extra syllables for pitches not within the key signature) to deal with any momentary key changes that occur.

Jazz musicians and educators often prefer the second approach for standards, as the key signature of the tune still exerts a significant influence over the song as a whole (most typically in the melody), even though momentary key changes may occur in the harmony. More on momentary keys is coming in Chapter 18.

CHROMATIC SOLFEGE AND RESOLUTIONS IN MINOR KEYS

Diatonic solfege works fine if we stay within a major key, but we'll need to introduce syllables for the other (chromatic) pitches if we are in a minor key, or if we use the fixed DO approach outlined above. Chromatic solfege syllables have enharmonically equivalent names, similar to enharmonic note names for sharps and flats. For example, the notes C♯ and D♭ are the same pitch, but we would use one name or the other depending on whether we were actually sharping the note C or flatting the note D. Similarly, we will use a different chromatic solfege syllable if we are sharping DO than we will if we are flatting RE. This concept will then work in all keys. The following examples show all of the chromatic solfege syllables, in between the diatonic solfege syllables (and with DO still assigned to C).

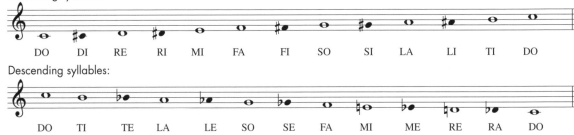

Note that the syllables for the sharped pitches all end with the vowel "i," pronounced "ee" (as in "dee," "ree," etc.), and that the syllables for the flatted pitches end with the vowel "e," pronounced "ay" (as in "tay," "lay," etc.)—with the exception of the flatted RE which becomes RA (pronounced "rah"). Again, don't forget that this works in all keys (not just C)!

In Chapter 9 we derived all of the minor scales (natural, harmonic, melodic) and saw how they were used within a minor key. In the next section we'll take a closer look at these scales from a chromatic-solfege point of view. We'll start with the harmonic minor scale, as this scale is a uniquely important source for the active-to-resting resolutions within a minor key, and will help us to develop the definitive II–V–I chord progression in minor. Later we'll use the melodic and natural minor scales to derive useful alternative options for the I chord.

Here is the harmonic minor scale built from the tonic of C, with solfege syllables attached (including chromatic syllables where needed):

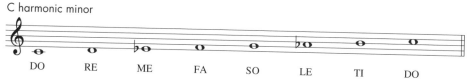

When comparing this harmonic minor scale to the major scale shown earlier, we can see that:

- ME (the flatted 3rd degree) has replaced MI (the 3rd degree).
- LE (the flatted 6th degree) has replaced LA (the 6th degree).

ME replaces MI in all of the minor scales, and ME therefore becomes an important new resting tone in a minor key. LE enables us to resolve into the resting tone SO by a half step (which was not possible in a major key), therefore LE becomes an important new active tone in a minor key. TI is still as active in minor as it was in major (i.e., resolving up to DO) and enables us to derive a dominant chord (containing a major 3rd above the root) built from SO, to lead back to the tonic—more about this in a moment.

Whether the minor scale degrees are in all the minor scales (like ME) or in just some of them (LE is only in the natural and harmonic minor scales, and TI is only in the harmonic and melodic minor scales), we can still use these scale degrees as needed within a minor key, as a whole, without worrying about which minor scale each particular scale degree may have come from. Believe it or not, this makes life much easier!

So the main active and resting properties for minor keys and minor scale degrees can be summarized as follows:

- DO, ME, and SO are resting tones of the minor scales.
- RE and FA are mildly active, as they resolve down to adjacent resting tones by whole steps. (Although RE can resolve up to ME by a half step, this resolution is not as strong as the other half-step resolutions.)
- LE is very active, as it resolves down by half step to an adjacent resting tone (SO).
- TI is very active (just like it is in major), as it resolves up to the tonic (DO) by a half step.

We can therefore say that the main active-to-resting resolutions within a minor key are:

- RE down to DO (by whole step);
- FA down to ME (by whole step);
- LE down to SO (by half step);
- TI up to DO (by half step).

You can listen to these minor-key resolutions on **Track 57**.

DO   RE – DO   FA – ME   LE – SO   TI – DO

For completeness we should add a couple more scale degree properties available within the natural and melodic minor scales:

- TE (the flatted 7th degree from the natural minor scale) is mildly active, as it can resolve up to DO by a whole step.
- LA (the 6th degree from the melodic minor scale) is mildly active, as it can resolve down to SO by a whole step (in the same way it does in a major key).

THE II–V–I PROGRESSION IN MINOR KEYS

Phew! Now that all that's out of the way, we can use these new scale degrees to create definitive II–V–I progressions in minor keys. When creating the II–V–I progression in minor, there are two guiding principles we should bear in mind:

1) The resulting chords should sound different than their major counterparts (for example, the II chord in minor should sound different from the II chord in major).

2) The movement between chords should make good use of the active-to-resting resolutions in minor, and in particular the new LE–SO half-step resolution (which was not present in major).

Because the harmonic minor scale is a useful source of active-to-resting resolutions, we'll start with that scale to build the II, V, and I chords in a minor key.

II chord: If we start from the note D (RE) and build a four-part chord, we get D–F–A♭–C (RE–FA–LE–DO). This spells a Dm7♭5 chord, which differs from Dm7 (II in major). Also, the chord contains A♭ (LE), a useful extra active tone of the II chord in minor.

V chord: If we start from the note G (SO) and build a four-part chord, we get G–B–D–F (SO–TI–RE–FA). This spells a G7 chord, which is the same thing we would get in major. However, if we extend this to a five-part chord by adding A♭ (LE), we get a G7♭9 chord, which is a recognizably different sound compared to the V in major. Also, the chord contains A♭ (LE), a useful extra active tone in the V chord in minor.

I chord: If we start from the note C (DO) and build a four-part chord, we get C–E♭–G–B (DO–ME–SO–TI). This spells a Cm(maj7) chord, which is different from Cmaj7 (I in major). Also, the chord contains E♭ (ME), a definitive resting tone of the I chord in minor.

So far so good, but now we need to develop some alternatives for the I chord in minor, and for this we'll look at the other minor scales. Earlier, when deriving the II–V–I in major, we saw that the major sixth chord was an alternative tonic chord to the major seventh chord. Similarly, for the tonic chord in minor, the minor sixth chord is an alternative to the minor/major seventh chord. We can derive both of these chords from the melodic minor scale.

DO   RE   ME   FA   SO   LA   TI   DO

Within this C melodic minor scale, if we start from the note C (DO) and build a four-part chord, we again get C–E♭–G–B (DO–ME–SO–TI), which spells a Cm(maj7) chord. If we build a sixth chord, instead of a seventh chord, we get C–E♭–G–A (DO–ME–SO–LA) which spells a Cm6 chord. In jazz these two chords are often used interchangeably as tonic chords in a minor key. This is similar to the use of the major seventh and major sixth chords as tonic chords in major keys.

But wait... there's more! Unfortunately, it's not quite enough to have just these forms of the I chord in minor. Both of them will sound jazzy and somewhat angular (the minor with major seventh chord, in particular). Consequently, for more commercial or pop styles, we'll need the option of using a minor seventh as the tonic chord. We can derive this chord from the natural minor scale:

DO   RE   ME   FA   SO   LE   TE   DO

Within this C natural minor scale, if we start from the note C (DO) and build a four-part chord, we get C–E♭–G–B♭ (DO–ME–SO–TE), which spells a Cm7 chord.

Okay, here's where we're at with all these II–V–I progressions in minor keys:

- The II chord in minor keys is invariably a IIm7♭5 across the range of jazz styles. There are no common alternative forms that you need to be concerned with (phew!).

- The most basic and definitive choice for the V chord in minor is the V7♭9 chord. More broadly, all altered dominant chords can function as V chords in minor keys. (See Chapters 11 and 16 for more information about altered dominant chords.)

- The I chord in minor has some different forms. The Im(maj7) (found in the melodic and harmonic minor scales) and its close cousin the Im6 chord (found in the melodic minor scale) both impart a jazzy and sophisticated sound. For more straightforward pop applications, go with the Im7 chord (found in the natural minor scale).

Let's now have a listen to these II–V–I chord options in minor:

Track 57
(0:19)

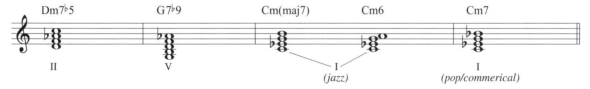

When deriving the II–V–I progression in major, we focused on the definitive tones, which were the thirds and sevenths of each chord (refer to **Track 56**, section starting 0:32). Now, for the II–V–I progression in minor the definitive tones include not only the thirds and sevenths, but also the altered fifth and altered ninth. (The fifth or ninth does not impart any definition to the chord unless it is altered.) Following are the definitive tones of the II–V–I progression in C minor, first with the progression ending on the Im(maj7) chord.

Track 57
(0:35)

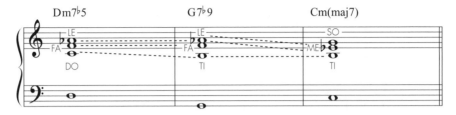

And now here's another version with the progression ending on the Im7 chord:

Track 57
(0:45)

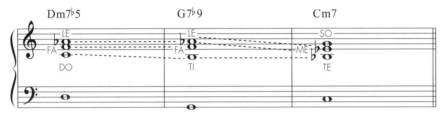

We can make the following observations about these II–V–I progressions in minor (compare these examples to those on **Track 56**, section starting 0:32):

- The third and seventh of each chord (together with the altered fifth of the first chord and altered ninth of the second), define the IIm7♭5, V7♭9, Im(maj7) chord qualities.
- This progression enables us to move between DO and TI (from IIm7♭5 to V7♭9), between FA and ME, and LE and SO [from V7♭9 to Im(maj7)]. All these movements (especially the LE–SO resolution) effectively define the minor key center to our ear.
- The root movement of the II–V–I progression (D–G–C) uses a strong leading circle-of-fifths motion, just like in the major key.

Next we'll look at the Latin jazz standard "Black Orpheus" to check out some II–V–I harmony used in a minor key (and its relative major key). As we did in "Misty," we'll see partial II–V–I progressions. Here's a leadsheet excerpt from this song:

Black Orpheus

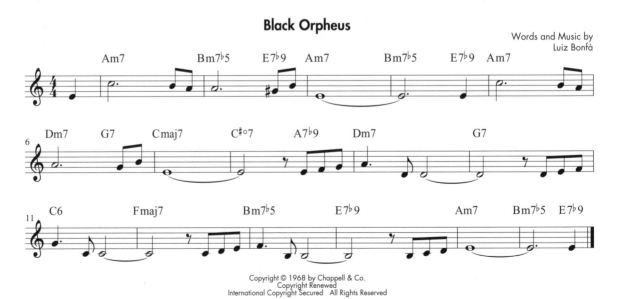

Notice that in measures 2–3, 4–5, and 13–15 of "Black Orpheus" we have II–V–I progressions in A minor (Bm7♭5–E7♭9–Am7). Then in measures 6–7 and 9–11 we have II–V–I progressions in C major, which is the relative major of A minor. This type of harmonic movement (between the relative major and minor) is common in both jazz and pop styles. Also, in measures 8–9 we have a V–I progression in D minor (A7♭9–Dm7) with the Dm7 chord then becoming the II chord of C major. This Dm7 chord is therefore a linking chord that functions in both the preceding and following momentary keys (D minor and C major).

Besides the II–V–I chords in minor and major, this example has some substitute chords.
- The C♯°7 chord in measure 8 can be considered a substitute for an A7♭9 chord (a VII-for-V substitution in the key of D minor).
- The Fmaj7 chord in measure 12 can be considered a substitute for a Dm7 chord (a IV-for-II substitution in the key of C major).

Chapter 13 is full of more information about substitute relationships.

COMBINING II–V–I PROGRESSIONS FROM MAJOR AND MINOR KEYS

So far we have been using II–V–I progressions from a major or minor key only (for example, Dm7–G7–Cmaj7 in the key of C major, or Dm7♭5–G7♭9–Cm7 in the key of C minor). However, II–V–I chords from major and minor keys can be mixed freely. For example, we might use the II chord from C major (Dm7), followed by a V chord in C minor (G7♭9), followed by a I chord from C major (Cmaj7). This type of mixing is very common in jazz. Let's now take a look at an excerpt from the famous jazz standard "Autumn Leaves" that uses this technique:

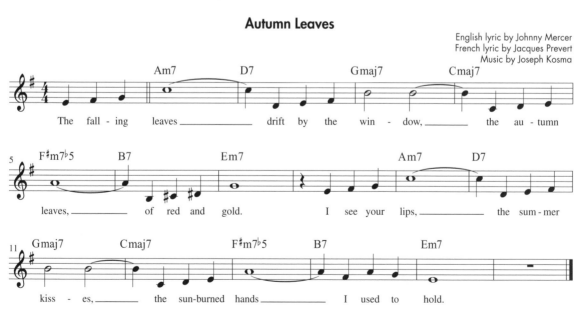

Autumn Leaves

English lyric by Johnny Mercer
French lyric by Jacques Prevert
Music by Joseph Kosma

In measures 1–3 of "Autumn Leaves" we have a II–V–I in G major (Am7–D7–Gmaj7). In measures 5–8 we have a mixed II–V–I progression (from the keys of E minor and E major). The F#m7♭5 is a II chord in E minor, the B7 chord is a V chord in E major (as this dominant chord is not altered), and the Em7 chord is a I chord in E minor. An altered ninth of this B7 chord would have clashed with the melody, which contains the unaltered ninth of the B7 chord (C#) on beat 3 of the measure. The harmonic structure in measures 1–8 is then repeated for measures 9–16.

"Autumn Leaves" is one of the most-recorded jazz standards of all time. The song originated in France (where it was known as *Les feuilles mortes*) with the music written by Joseph Kosma. English lyrics were then added by the American songwriter Johnny Mercer in the late 1940s. The song was featured in the 1956 movie *Autumn Leaves*, starring Joan Crawford, with Nat King Cole singing the title sequence. A virtual "who's who" of jazz luminaries have performed and recorded the song, including Louis Armstrong, Cannonball Adderley, Bill Evans, Miles Davis, Oscar Peterson, Joe Henderson, and Chet Baker.

CHAPTER 13
CHORD SUBSTITUTIONS

What's Ahead:

- Substitutions for the II–V–I chords in major
- Substitutions for the II–V–I chords in minor
- Tritone substitutions and approach chords

SUBSTITUTIONS FOR THE II–V–I CHORDS IN MAJOR

In the last chapter we derived the definitive II, V, and I chords in a major key. (Just a reminder: in the key of C these chords are Dm7, G7, and Cmaj7 or C6, which you can find on **Track 56**.) These are considered primary chords in the key, but there are other available four-part chords that can act as substitutes for them. For a chord to be able to substitute for a primary chord, it will need to have notes in common with that primary chord and, in particular, it will need to share the same active or resting characteristics, as explained in

the last chapter. We'll start with the II chord in C major (expanded to its five-part form: Dm9) and look at the upper part of this chord to see if a suitable substitute can be derived.

Notice that the top four notes of the five-part II chord (Dm9) form an Fmaj7 four-part chord. This Fmaj7 chord (a IV chord) has several notes in common with the original Dm9 chord, including the important active tone FA. (In Chapter 12, we saw how FA resolved to MI across the II–V–I progression in major.) So we can consider this IV chord to be a substitute for the II chord in major. This means that (subject to context) we can either substitute the IV chord for the II chord, or replace the IV chord with the original definitive II chord. This will change the vertical quality of the chord and the root movement of the progression (i.e., the intervals between the roots of successive chords), but it will preserve the active quality within the key.

The two songs at the end of Chapter 12 both contained IV chords in major keys (which could be considered substitutes for II chords). Check out the Fmaj7 chord in measure 12 of "Black Orpheus," and the Cmaj7 chords in measures 4 and 12 of "Autumn Leaves."

Track 58
(0:07) Next up is the V chord in C major (expanded to its five-part form: G9). We'll look once again at the upper part of this chord to derive a substitute.

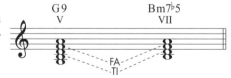

Notice that the top four notes of the five-part V chord (G9) form a Bm7♭5 four-part chord. This VII chord has several notes in common with the original V chord, including the important active tones TI and FA. So we can consider the VII chord to be a substitute for the V chord in major. This means that (subject to context) we can either substitute the VII chord for the V chord, or replace the VII chord with the original definitive V chord.

It turns out that the I chord in major has two available diatonic substitutes. To derive the first one, we'll expand the Cmaj7 form of the I chord to the five-part Cmaj9 chord.

Notice that the top four notes of the five-part I chord (Cmaj9) form an Em7 four-part chord. This III chord has several notes in common with the original I chord, including the important resting tone MI. So we can consider the III chord to be a substitute for the I chord in major. This means that (subject to context) we can either substitute the III chord for the I chord, or replace the III chord with the original definitive I chord.

To derive the second substitute, we'll now take the four-part C6 form of the I chord and invert it, placing the sixth in the bass.

Notice that the four notes of this I chord (C6) have been rearranged to form an Am7 four-part chord. This VI chord has all four notes in common with the original I chord, including the important resting tone MI. So we can consider the VI chord to be a substitute for the I chord in major. This means that (subject to context) we can either substitute the VI chord for the I chord, or replace the VI chord with the original definitive I chord.

Although we started out with different forms of the I chord (i.e., Cmaj9 and C6) to derive the last two examples, in practice the III-for-I and VI-for-I substitutions will work for all four- and five-part forms of the I chord (i.e., Cmaj7, C6, Cmaj9, C_9^6, etc.). Because the VI chord is a little more restful within the key than the III chord, the VI-for-I substitution is used more commonly than the III-for-I.

Now it's time to summarize these chord-substitution relationships in major keys. The primary II, V, and I chords are shown above the staff and the substitute chords are shown below the staff.

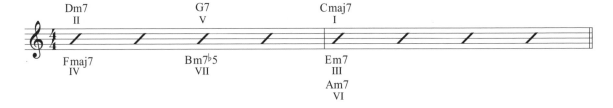

- The IV chord can substitute for the II chord.
- The VII chord can substitute for the V chord.
- The III or VI chord can substitute for the I chord.

Now we'll see some of these chord substitutions at work in the popular Roberta Flack song "Killing Me Softly with His Song":

Killing Me Softly with His Song

Words by Norman Gimbel
Music by Charles Fox

This song contains a good example of a VI-for-I substitution in a major key. In measures 1–3 we have a II–V–I progression in A♭ (B♭m7–E♭9–A♭maj7). In measures 5–6 we repeat the same II–V progression, but instead of going to the I chord in measure 7, we use the VI chord (Fm7) as a substitute. Additionally, the D♭maj7 chord in measure 4 is a IV chord which can be considered a IV-for-II substitution in A♭.

SUBSTITUTIONS FOR THE II–V–I CHORDS IN MINOR

In the last chapter we also derived the definitive II–V–I chords in a minor key. (Just a reminder: In the key of C minor these chords are Dm7♭5, G7♭9, and Cm(maj7) or Cm6 or Cm7, which you

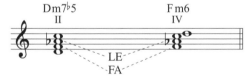

can find on **Track 57**.) We'll now derive substitutes that share the same active or resting qualities as these primary chords. We begin with the II chord in C minor (Dm7♭5), inverted so that the third is in the bass.

Notice that the four notes of this II chord (Dm7♭5) have been rearranged to form an Fm6 (IV chord). This chord has all of the notes in common with the original II chord, including the important active tones LE and FA. (In Chapter 12 we saw how FA resolved to ME, and LE resolved to SO, across the II–V–I progression in minor.) So we can consider this IV chord to be a substitute for the II chord in minor. This means that (subject to context) we can either substitute the IV chord for the II chord, or replace the IV chord with the original definitive II chord.

Next up is the five-part V chord in C minor (G7♭9). Again, we'll look at the upper part of this chord to derive a suitable substitute.

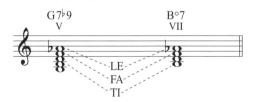

Notice that the top four notes of the five-part V chord (G7♭9) form a B°7 four-part chord. This VII chord has several notes in common with the original V chord, including the important active tones TI, FA, and LE. So we can consider this VII chord to be a substitute for the V chord in minor. This means that (subject to context) we can either substitute the VII chord for the V chord, or replace the VII chord with the original definitive V chord.

Track 59
(0:14)

As in a major key, the I chord in minor also has two substitutes available. One of these will apply to the jazzy forms of the I chord [Im(maj7) or Im6], and the other will apply to the pop form of the I chord (Im7). To derive the first substitute, we'll take the Cm6 form of the I chord and invert it, placing the sixth in the bass.

Notice that the four notes of this Cm6 I chord have been rearranged to form an Am7♭5 chord. This VI chord has all four notes in common with the original I chord, including the important resting tone ME. So we can consider this VI chord to be a substitute for the jazzy forms of the I chord in minor [i.e., Cm(maj7), Cm6, Cm9(maj7), Cm⁶₉]. This means that (subject to context) we can either substitute the VI chord for this type of I chord, or replace the VI chord with the original definitive I chord.

Track 59
(0:21)

To derive the second substitute, we'll expand the Cm7 form of the I chord to the five-part Cm9 chord.

Notice that the top four notes of the five-part I chord (Cm9) form a four-part E♭maj7 (III chord). This chord has several notes in common with the original I chord, including the important resting tone ME. So we can consider this III chord to be a substitute for the pop forms of the I chord in minor (i.e., Cm7, Cm9). This means that (subject to context) we can either substitute the III chord for this type of I chord, or replace the III chord with the original definitive I chord.

Now it's time to summarize these chord-substitution relationships in minor keys. The primary II, V, and I chords are shown above the staff and the substitute chords are shown below the staff.

- The IV chord can substitute for the II chord.
- The VII chord can substitute for the V chord.
- The VI chord can substitute for the jazzy forms of the I chord.
- The III chord can substitute for the pop forms of the I chord.

Let's see some of these chord substitutions at work, first in the Cole Porter song "I Love You."

I Love You
from MEXICAN HAYRIDE

Words and Music by
Cole Porter

This song contains a good example of a IV-for-II substitution in a minor key. In measures 1–2 we have a IV–V progression in F minor (B♭m6–C7♭9). The B♭m6 is a substitute for the II chord (Gm7♭5). (This substitution is often shown on leadsheets for this song—although the Gm7♭5 that's hiding underneath this B♭m6 chord symbol sounds pretty good too!) This leads to an Fmaj7 chord in measure 3 (recall Chapter 12, where we saw that II–V–I progressions in major and minor can be freely mixed together). We also have a II–V–I progression in G minor in measures 4–5, linking into a "mixed" II–V–I progression in F minor and F major in measures 5–8.

Ten More Cole Porter Songs You Should Know

Cole Porter is one of the most celebrated composers and songwriters of all time. Like his contemporaries George Gershwin and Irving Berlin, he wrote many Broadway shows and songs, although his greatest successes did not come until his middle and later years. Many of his contributions to the "Great American Songbook" have been performed and recorded by successive generations of jazz musicians, notably including John Coltrane's version of "I Love You" on the album *Lush Life*. Here are ten more of his works that you should check out:

"Let's Do It (Let's Fall in Love)"   "I Get a Kick Out of You"
"You Do Something to Me"   "Begin the Beguine"
"What Is This Thing Called Love?"   "Just One of Those Things"
"Night and Day"   "Easy To Love"
"Love for Sale"   "Always True to You (In My Fashion)"

Cole Porter

Next we'll look at the jazz standard "It Could Happen to You," written by Jimmy Van Heusen in the 1940s.

It Could Happen to You
from the Paramount Picture AND THE ANGELS SING

Words by Johnny Burke
Music by James Van Heusen

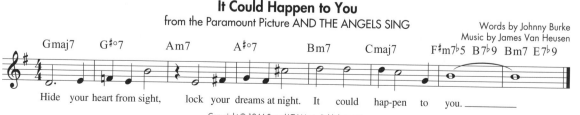

"It Could Happen to You" has some good examples of VII-for-V substitutions in minor keys. In measures 2–3 we have a VII–I progression in A minor (G#°7–Am7), in which the G#°7 is a substitute for the V chord (E7♭9). Similarly, in measures 4–5 we have a VII–I progression in B minor (A#°7–Bm7), with the A#°7 substituting for the V chord (F#7♭9). (These substitutions are often shown on leadsheets for this song, although the "original" E7♭9 and F#7♭9 chords work fine as well.) We also have a II–V progression in E minor in measure 7, and a mixed II–V progression in A major/minor in measure 8.

TRITONE SUBSTITUTIONS FOR DOMINANT CHORDS

Next we'll check out a chord-substitution technique known as *tritone substitution*, which is common across a wide range of jazz and jazz-influenced styles. This involves replacing a dominant chord with another dominant chord whose root is a tritone (an augmented 4th or diminished 5th) away from the root of the original chord. This is most often done within a II–V–I progression, or a partial II–V–I (i.e., just the V–I). In order for this technique to work, the melody at that point in the tune has to fit within the replacement dominant chord. Let's first of all look at the II–V–I progression in C major (isolating the definitive thirds and sevenths of each chord, as we did on **Track 56**), and see how this technique would be applied to the G7 dominant chord.

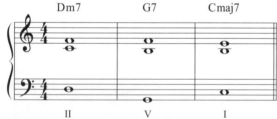 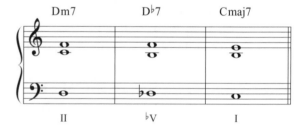

In the second three-measure example above, we have replaced the G7 chord with a D♭7 chord. The root of the substitute dominant chord (D♭) is a tritone away from the root of the original dominant chord (G). Notice that, between these two chords, the third and seventh "stay the same"—actually the third of the G7 chord (B) becomes the seventh of the D♭7 chord and the seventh of the G7 chord (F) becomes the third of the D♭7 chord. Because of this, the movement of these 7–3 lines (by half steps and common tones) across the II–V–I progression is not altered as a result of the tritone substitution, which makes this substitution uniquely useful in jazz styles.

Next we'll see this technique at work in another famous jazz standard, "All the Things You Are" by Jerome Kern. Following are the first sixteen measures of the song showing the basic definitive chord changes most commonly used.

All the Things You Are

To implement this tritone substitution, we look for a II–V–I progression and see if the melody on the V chord would also work over the substitute chord.

- The first II–V–I progression occurs in measures 2–4 in the key of A♭ (B♭m7–E♭7–A♭maj7). The tritone substitution for the E♭7 in measure 3 would be A7. The melody at this point is G (the third of E♭7), which would also work over the A7 substitute chord, where it would become the seventh of this chord.

- The second II–V–I progression is in measures 10–12 (Fm7–B♭7–E♭maj7) in the momentary key of E♭. The tritone substitution for the B♭7 in measure 11 would be E7. The melody at this point is D (the third of B♭7), which would work over the E7 substitute chord, as it would become the seventh of this chord.

Here is the same section of the song with these tritone substitutions applied:

All the Things You Are

It would also be technically possible to employ this substitution technique within the V–I progressions in measures 6–7 (G7–Cmaj7) and 14–15 (D7–Gmaj7). However, if we replaced the G7 in measure 6 with a D♭7, we would have no root movement between measures 5 and 6 (i.e., from D♭maj7 to D♭7), which sounds less interesting and attractive. A similar situation happens in measures 14–15.

DOMINANT APPROACH CHORDS

This is a chord-embellishment technique that is related to the previous topic. A *dominant approach chord* is an extra dominant chord inserted into a progression, one whose root approaches the root of the following chord by a descending half step. This chord movement is similar to that of the tritone substitute chord in the previous examples, but with the following differences:

- The chord being approached can be a major, minor, or dominant chord (i.e., we are not limited to approaching major chords).
- The new approach chord "steals" part of the measure (typically the last one or two beats) from the chord originally preceding the target.

To apply this technique, we look at each of the chord changes in the song and figure out what the dominant approach chord would be (i.e., the dominant chord with a root a half step higher than the chord in question). We then look at the melody notes immediately preceding the chord to see if they would fit over the new dominant approach chord. If so, we can then insert the new approach chord below these melody notes, "stealing" one or more beats from the chord. "All the Things You Are" presents several opportunities to do this, as we will see.

All the Things You Are

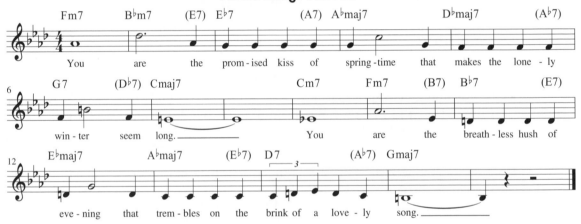

The various approach chords have been added as follows:

- Looking at the E♭7 in measure 3, the dominant approach into this would be E7. The melody note on beat 4 of the preceding measure is A♭ (equivalent to G♯), which is the third of E7. We can therefore insert the E7 as a dominant approach chord on beat 4 of measure 2, leading into the E♭7 in measure 3.

- Looking at the A♭maj7 in measure 4, the dominant approach into this would be A7. The melody note on beat 4 of the preceding measure is G, which is the seventh of A7. We can therefore insert A7 as a dominant approach chord on beat 4 of measure 3, leading into the A♭maj7 in measure 4.

- Similar logic applies to the remaining added dominant approach chords, leading into measures 6, 7, 11, 12, 14, and 15.

As with all types of embellishment, don't overdo it! Although this song allows for numerous dominant approach chords to be added, you probably shouldn't use this technique at every opportunity, as it could become distracting. Deployed with restraint and taste, however, these approach chords can certainly spice up your jazz arranging and performing.

CHAPTER 14

SONG FORM AND STRUCTURE

> **What's Ahead:**
> - Sections of a song
> - Common song forms
> - Classical forms

SECTIONS OF A SONG

Whether you're writing your own songs or listening to somebody else's, you should be aware of the different sections that together make up the form of the song (such as the intro, verse, chorus, bridge, etc.). First we'll discuss form in contemporary popular styles of vocal and instrumental music. And then we'll conclude the chapter with an introduction to some commonly occurring forms in classical music.

There are many different ways to combine sections within a song, as we will see shortly. Some sections can be labeled alphabetically (i.e., "A," "B," and so on)—here's where you can impress your musician friends by telling them that your new song has an "AABA" form! Jazz musicians often use this system of letters to refer to the parts of a tune. Letters can also be used to describe the form of a pop song, though labels like "verse" and "chorus" are more common. In this chapter we'll look at some song forms in both pop and jazz styles.

We begin by examining the various sections that may appear within a pop song:

INTRO

The *intro* (if there is one) to a contemporary song is normally an instrumental section that sets the groove and mood. The chord progression is typically borrowed from another part of the song (such as the verse or chorus) and any melody or instrumental hook is likely to return later on. Intros in commercial pop styles are mostly short (four or eight measures) and lead directly to the verse or chorus.

VERSE

The *verse* in vocal songs is normally where the lyric "tells the story." Most vocal songs have two or more verses, usually with different sets of lyrics. In contemporary styles the verse leads into the chorus (or the pre-chorus, if there is one) and is often at a lower intensity level than these other sections of the song. The verse can also be referred to as an "A" section within the form.

PRE-CHORUS (SET-UP)

The *pre-chorus* (if present) is an extra section of a vocal song, added between the verse and the chorus. The pre-chorus is sometimes called the set-up. The function of the pre-chorus is to add momentum and energy in building toward the chorus. Pre-choruses, like intros, are normally short (again, four or eight measures is typical). The melody and chord progression used in the pre-chorus are often different from those of both the verse and chorus. The pre-chorus can also be referred to as a "B" section within the form. Later in this chapter we'll look at "Shattered Dreams," by Johnny Hates Jazz, which has a great example of a pre-chorus.

CHORUS

The *chorus* is the section of the song with the most energy and intensity. Melodically the chorus normally contains a repeated section, or *hook*, designed to get the listener's attention. Lyrically the chorus will contain the "main message" of the song, which is often reflected in the song's title. This is the part of the song that most listeners or fans are most likely to remember. The chorus can also be referred to as a "B" section within the form (or a "C" section if it follows a pre-chorus).

BRIDGE

The *bridge* (if present) normally occurs after the second chorus of the song and provides contrast and variation before leading back into another verse or chorus. The lyrics here often introduce another element to the story, or tell it from a different angle. Musically, the melodic and/or harmonic material normally differs from that of the verse and chorus. The bridge can also be referred to as a "C" section (or a "D" section if a pre-chorus is present). One of the most effective pop-music bridges ever written is in the song "Every Breath You Take" by the Police.

INSTRUMENTAL SECTION OR SOLO

Many vocal songs will feature an instrumental section or solo to change the focus and build excitement. An instrumental solo will generally be improvised over the chord progression from the verse or chorus, whereas an instrumental section is a composed melody part added to the song. Highly regarded instrumental solos (which have greatly enhanced their songs' popularity) include Bobby Keys' sax solo on the Rolling Stones' "Brown Sugar" and Eddie Van Halen's guitar solo on Michael Jackson's "Beat It." Great examples of composed instrumental sections are found in Nik Kershaw's "Wouldn't It Be Good" and Peter Gabriel's "Sledgehammer."

ENDING (OR CODA)

Most recordings of pop songs will fade out over repetitions of the chorus, but for live performances—and even on some recordings—an actual ending is used. This might be as simple as ending the song (typically on a I chord) after the last chorus, or it might involve an extra ending section (*coda*) based on an earlier part of the song. Some artists will add an extended instrumental ending using different material, which then becomes a special feature in its own right. Memorable examples of this occur in Eric Clapton's "Layla" (from *Layla and Other Assorted Love Songs* by Derek and the Dominos) and "Speedway at Nazareth" by Mark Knopfler.

COMMON SONG FORMS

Now we'll look at some famous popular songs and analyze their forms. First up is Elton John's "Candle in the Wind," which is based on a verse–chorus form (which we can also call an "AB" form). This means that the verse–chorus (or "AB") unit is repeated throughout the song.

This chart is written in cut time (equivalent to 2/2 time), which means there are two half-note beats per measure. In reality, this tune has a sixteenth-note feel; but instead of the chart being written in 4/4 time using sixteenth notes, it has been written in cut time using eighth notes—with twice the number of measures. For example, the verse is sixteen cut-time measures long, which would be equivalent to eight measures of 4/4 time. You will sometimes see this notational technique in pop fakebooks. This is done to aid readability (on the supposition that eighth notes are easier to read than sixteenth notes)—but don't forget that the measures go by twice as fast!

Candle in the Wind

Words and Music by
Elton John and Bernie Taupin

"Candle in the Wind" has an "AB" (or verse–chorus) form.
- The verse (or "A" section) is sixteen measures long. Two lines of lyrics are shown (for verses 1 and 2). On the third repeat of the form, the lyrics from the first verse are used again.
- The chorus (or "B" section) is seventeen measures long (the result of adding an extra measure toward the end of a sixteen-measure phrase). After the third repeat of the form, half the chorus is repeated again, creating an end section (or coda).

The leadsheet for "Candle in the Wind" includes some slash chord symbols.
- The E/G♯ symbol means an E major triad placed over its third (G♯).
- The A/E symbol means an A major triad placed over its fifth (E).

You'll find more about slash chords in Chapter 19.

"Candle in the Wind" is one of Elton John's most famous songs. It was written (with John's longtime lyricist Bernie Taupin) in 1973 and was included on the *Goodbye Yellow Brick Road* album of the same year. Originally inspired by the life of Marilyn Monroe, the song was reworked in 1997 as a tribute to Diana, Princess of Wales. The CD single of this version became the second-best-selling single in history (eclipsed only by Bing Crosby's "White Christmas").

Photo by George DeSota/Redferns

Elton John

Next we'll look at the pop/rock tune "Shattered Dreams" from the British band Johnny Hates Jazz. This is based on a verse/pre-chorus/chorus form (which we can call "ABC"). Again, this means that the form is repeated as necessary during the song.

Shattered Dreams

Words and Music by
Clark Datchler

This song has an "ABC" (or verse–set-up–chorus) form.

- The verse (or "A" section) is eight measures long. Two lines of lyrics are shown (for verses 1 and 2).
- The pre-chorus (or "B" section) is four measures long. This is a short section that builds energy and momentum into the chorus. Two lines of lyrics are shown (for pre-chorus 1 and 2).
- The chorus (or "C" section) is eight measures long.

It is typical for pop music forms to be varied (sections repeated, key changes added, and so on) for commercial recording purposes. These can be considered arrangement techniques that are applied to the original structure of the song. The recording of "Shattered Dreams" is a good example of this. Although the basic structure of this song is an "ABC" form, on the recorded version the chorus is repeated on the second time through the form. This is followed by a short instrumental section leading to a repeat of the pre-chorus and chorus (now transposed up by a half step). This all helps to increase the song's impact and radio appeal.

origins

Johnny Hates Jazz was a British pop/rock trio that will forever be known in the US for the hit single "Shattered Dreams." The band was primarily a vehicle for the vocal and songwriting talents of Clark Datchler. The group's big break came when they were signed by Virgin Records in 1986—ironically on the strength of a performance at a jazz club!

Photo by Martina Raddatz/Redferns

Johnny Hates Jazz

Our next song is the famous Disney classic "Beauty and the Beast," by Alan Menken. This is based on a verse–chorus–bridge form with a twist: The bridge has a built-in key change (from E♭ major to F major). Following the bridge, the verse and chorus is repeated in the new key. So to indicate the form fully, we could use the letters "ABCAB" (the last A and B sections being in the new key).

Beauty and the Beast
from Walt Disney's BEAUTY AND THE BEAST

Lyrics by Howard Ashman
Music by Alan Menken

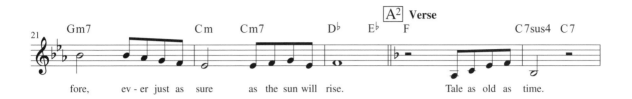

This song has an "ABCAB" (or verse–chorus–bridge–verse–chorus) form.
- The first verse (or "A" section) is eight measures long.
- The first chorus (or "B" section) is also eight measures long. It starts similarly to the verse, but then builds in intensity, ending with the song title in the lyric.
- The bridge (or "C" section) contrasts with the preceding sections. It is seven measures long and transitions into the key of F major. The unusual phrase length and the key change combine to create an effective build into the next verse.
- The second verse (or "A" section) is again eight measures long, in the new key.
- The second chorus (or "B" section) is also eight measures long with an extra tag of three measures added at the end.

Now we're going to look at some song forms typically used in jazz tunes and standards. When analyzing these jazz song forms, musicians are more likely to use just letter names for the sections (i.e., "AABA"), rather than terms such as "verse," "chorus," and so on. Our first example is the well-known standard "Body and Soul," which uses the "AABA" form.

Body and Soul

Words by Edward Heyman, Robert Sour and Frank Eyton
Music by John Green

This song has an "AABA" form with each section being eight measures long (making thirty-two measures in total). Notice that measures 9–16 (the second "A" section) are a repeat of measures 1–8 (the first "A" section). Then measures 17–24 (the "B" section) have different harmonic and melodic material, leading into measures 25–32 (the last "A" section) which repeats the first section once more.

Some More "AABA" Jazz Standards You Should Know

"AABA" is the most popular song form for mainstream jazz and standards. Here are six more "AABA" classics that you should have in your collection:

- Herbie Hancock, "Maiden Voyage"
- Duke Ellington, "Satin Doll"
- Miles Davis, "Nardis"
- Thelonious Monk, "Well, You Needn't"
- Duke Ellington, "Take the 'A' Train"
- Benny Golson, "Killer Joe"

Photo provided by Photofest

Duke Ellington

After the "AABA" form, the next most common song form in jazz is the "ABAC" form. As with the "AABA" form, most tunes using the "ABAC" form are thirty-two measures in length. Our next example is the Rodgers and Hart standard "My Romance."

My Romance
from JUMBO

Words by Lorenz Hart
Music by Richard Rodgers

"My Romance" has an "ABAC" form, with each section being eight measures long (making thirty-two measures in total). Note that measures 9–16 (the "B" section) contain different harmonic and melodic material than measures 1–8 (the first "A" section). However, measures 17–24 (the second "A" section) are a repeat of measures 1–8 (the first "A" section). Finally, measures 25–32 (the "C" section) contain different harmonic and melodic material from that of the other sections.

Some More "ABAC" Jazz Standards You Should Know

"ABAC" is also a popular song form for jazz and standards. Here are six more "ABAC" classics that you should check out:

- Jimmy Van Heusen, "I Thought About You"
- Jerome Kern, "Dearly Beloved"
- Miles Davis, "Four"
- Frank Loesser, "If I Were a Bell"
- Frank Churchill, "Someday My Prince Will Come"
- Nacio Herb Brown, "You Stepped Out of a Dream"

Photo courtesy of Culver Pictures

Jerome Kern

Now we'll switch gears and talk about the blues form. If you're jamming with your buddies and someone calls out "Let's play the blues in C," most likely this is the form you'll be using. Most blues songs have a twelve-measure form, which means that a twelve-measure chord progression is repeated for both the melody and the improvised solos. Our next example is a piano arrangement of the traditional blues song "C.C. Rider," a twelve-measure blues in the key of C.

C.C. Rider

Traditional

audio tracks 61

We can analyze the "C.C. Rider" blues progression as follows:
- The chords used are dominant sevenths built from the 1st, 4th, and 5th degrees of the key (C major), which we can refer to as the I7, IV7, and V7 chords.
- The twelve-measure sequence breaks down into three sections of four measures each.
- The first four measures normally use the I7 (C7 in this case). A common variation is to move to the IV7 (which would have been F7 in this case) in the second measure, returning to the I7 for measures 3–4.
- The next four measures (measures 5–8 of the form) begin with the IV7, normally returning to the I7 after two bars (i.e., in measure 7).
- The third four measures (measures 9–12 of the form) begin with the V7 (G7 in this case), typically followed by the IV7 (in measure 10), returning to the I7 in measure 11. Measures 11–12 then act as a turnaround section, leading back to the beginning of the form. Many chord progressions are possible here; the simplest options are to stay on the I7 or to move to the V7 in measure 12.

There are many variations on the blues progression, particularly in jazz/blues, where more substitutions and complex chords can be used. Also, although the twelve-measure form is predominant, other lengths are used as well:
- The eight-measure form is commonly found in New Orleans blues styles.
- The 24-measure form is used in some blues/rock and jazz/blues styles—in particular the jazz waltz, as we will see shortly.

Our next song example is the Ray Charles R&B classic "What'd I Say," which uses the basic twelve-measure blues form, this time in the key of F.

What'd I Say

Words and Music by
Ray Charles

Tell me what'd I say? Tell me what'd I say right now?

Tell me what'd I say?__ Tell me what'd I say?

Tell me what'd I say?__ Tell me what'd I say?

Note that this tune follows the basic twelve-measure blues form exactly, with the I7 (F7) on measure 1, the IV7 (B♭7) on measure 5, and the V7 (C7) on measure 9. The melody is simple, consisting of two-measure motifs that repeat and develop over the blues progression. Sparse and repetitive melodies are common in simpler blues styles.

Now we're going to look at a more sophisticated blues, a jazz/blues waltz with a 24-measure form. In Chapter 8 we learned that 3/4 time was also known as waltz time. The jazz/blues waltz is written in 3/4 time and typically doubles the number of measures in the blues form. Jazz/blues chord progressions are often much more involved than those of the basic blues, using various II–V progressions, substitute chords, and so on. We can see all this at work in "Bluesette," the famous jazz waltz written by Toots Thielemans.

Bluesette

Words by Norman Gimbel
Music by Jean Thielemans

Although this tune has many more chord changes than the basic blues, it is still loosely based on a 24-measure blues form in G major. The first eight-measure section begins with the Gmaj7 chord (instead of G7) and the second eight-measure section begins with Cmaj7 (instead of C7). As a variation, the last eight-measure section begins with an A♭maj7 chord and then moves through various II–V progressions toward the D7 chord.

Other notable jazz waltzes that use 24-measure blues forms include "All Blues" by Miles Davis and "Footprints" by Wayne Shorter.

CLASSICAL FORMS

Within the world of classical music, many different forms exist, such as the cantata, concerto, fugue, march, minuet, opera, oratorio, sonata, symphony, and various others. Each of these forms have a specific structure that the composer needs to be aware of. Here we'll meet three of the best-known forms.

CONCERTO

The *concerto* features a solo voice or instrument accompanied by a full orchestra. This form originated in the Baroque period and has been popular ever since. The majority of solo concertos have a three-movement form (fast, slow, fast).

Recommended Listening:

Maurice Ravel, *Piano Concerto for the Left Hand*
Johann Sebastian Bach, *Brandenburg Concerto No. 4 in G Major*
Peter Ilyich Tchaikovsky, *Piano Concerto No. 1 in B♭ Minor, Op. 23*

Peter Ilyich Tchaikovsky

SONATA

Most *sonatas* from the Classical period onward feature either solo piano or a piano accompanying another instrument (often violin or cello). Sonatas exist in one-, two-, three-, and four-movement forms, with four movements becoming the established norm in Beethoven's time.

Ludwig van Beethoven

Recommended Listening:

Ludwig van Beethoven, *Piano Sonata No. 8 in C Minor, Op. 13 ("Pathétique")*
Franz Liszt, *Piano Sonata in B minor*
John Cage, *Sonatas and Interludes for Prepared Piano*

SYMPHONY

The *symphony* is a large-scale orchestral work, traditionally with four separate movements. The symphony is the principal form of instrumental classical music and has been featured prominently in concert programs since the rise of professional orchestras in the early 19th century.

Recommended Listening:

Ludwig van Beethoven, *Symphony No. 3 in E♭ Major, Op. 55 ("Eroica")*
Antonín Dvořák, *Symphony No. 9 in E Minor, Op. 95 ("From the New World")*
Aaron Copland, *Symphony No. 3*

Antonín Dvořák

CHAPTER 15

CHARTS AND FOLLOWING THE ROADMAP

What's Ahead:
- Fakebooks, charts, and leadsheets
- Roadmap directions

FAKEBOOKS, CHARTS, AND LEADSHEETS

Now it's time to explore the fun world of *fakebooks*, *charts*, and *leadsheets*. A *chart* is a notated version of a song showing the melody and chord symbols, or just the chord symbols without the melody. A chart should also show the overall form and sections of the song (intro, verse, chorus, etc.), as well as any "roadmap" directions, which might include repeats of sections, *D.C.* (meaning go back to the beginning), *D.S.* (meaning go back to the "sign"), *To Coda* (when to go to the coda), and so on. (More about following roadmaps in a moment!) When presented with a chart, the musician will then improvise a part based on an understanding of the musical style.

You'll want to know some basic vocabulary:
- If the chart has melody and chord symbols, it is also referred to as a *leadsheet*. Many of the songs in this book are presented as leadsheets.
- A *fakebook* is a collection of leadsheets, normally in a particular style (i.e., pop/rock, jazz standards, etc.).
- If a chart just has chord symbols, it is also known as a *chord chart*. Chord charts are not normally published in books, but are prepared by musicians and bands as needed for rehearsal or performance.

A chord chart might consist of just chord symbols and slashes; this tells the musician to comp (accompany) according to the style, as in the following example:

The chord chart might also include specific rhythmic information, with the exact chord voicings still being left up to the player.

A leadsheet will include the melody as well as the chord symbols:

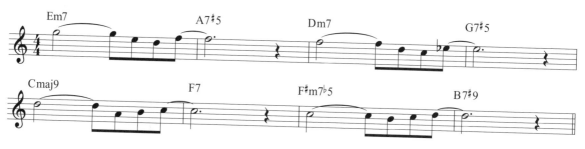

The individual charts in fakebooks are normally no longer than two pages, which makes them easy to use on the gig and means that each book can contain many different songs.

Ten Fakebooks You Should Know

Here are ten fakebooks that I use, grouped into three overall categories. Check out as many of them out as you can!

- *The Real Book, 6th ed.*

  The *Real Books* are the best-selling jazz books of all time. Since the 1970s, jazz musicians have trusted these volumes to get them through every gig, night after night. The problem is that the books were illegally produced and distributed, without any regard to copyright law, or royalties paid to the composers who created these musical masterpieces. Hal Leonard has published the first legitimate and legal editions of these books ever produced. The charts are clean, easy to read, and all of the notorious errors have been fixed. The 6th Edition remains true to the *Real Book* design, the song list is nearly identical, and the price for the Hal Leonard edition is even cheaper than the original!

- *The World's Greatest Fakebook* (contemporary and fusion jazz, mostly from the 1970s onward)
- *The New Real Book*, 3 vols. (vocal standards, classic and fusion jazz, Latin and Brazilian, some pop and soul standards in Volume 3)
- *The Standards Real Book* (vocal and jazz standards, some pop standards)
- *The All-Jazz Real Book* (classic and contemporary jazz, Latin and Brazilian)

  These are all Sher Music publications. Like many working pros, I think the Chuck Sher fakebooks really are state-of-the-art. They are meticulously transcribed, beautifully copied, and very easy to use. Any one of these books can provide a great education on how to notate and lay out a contemporary chart. Although the Sher fakebooks lean heavily toward jazz, *The Standards Real Book* and *The New Real Book, Volume 3* both have nice selections of pop songs.

- *The Ultimate Pop/Rock Fake Book* (Hal Leonard)
- *The Classic Rock Fake Book* (Hal Leonard)

  These books are good sources of pop and rock songs—good places to start if you are a beginner or are new to using fakebooks, as pop and rock tunes normally have easier chord progressions and melodies than the jazz repertoire.

ROADMAP DIRECTIONS

Now we'll learn how to navigate our way through a chart using roadmap directions. These conventions apply whether you're reading a leadsheet from a fakebook, printed sheet music with a piano arrangement, or a chord chart that you've prepared for a gig with your band. The following chord chart illustrates the basic roadmap directions that you'll need to be familiar with.

Roadmap Rock

By Mark Harrison

Let's take a tour through "Roadmap Rock" and see how we follow the roadmap.

- The first four measures (labeled "**Intro**") have *repeat signs* around them. To the left of measure 1, the *repeat sign* is the double barline with the two dots to the right. The matching repeat sign is at the end of measure 4 (the double barline with the two dots to the left). This means that we play these four measures and then repeat them (making eight measures total), before proceeding to the next section. These four measures contain rhythmic notation as well as chord symbols.

- The next section (starting at measure 5) has the rehearsal letter "A" attached and is also labeled "**Verse**." In practice, usually one or the other of these labeling methods will be used. Rehearsal letters (corresponding to the sections of the form) are convenient; you can call out "Let's take it from letter 'A'!" during rehearsal, which is often quicker than trying to find a measure number on the chart. Notice that this section is preceded by a "sign" (𝄋). This means that later on we're going to jump back to this point, via a "*D.S.*" (*dal segno*, meaning "from the sign") command. Also, we have a repeat sign to the left of measure 5, with its corresponding repeat sign further on in the next section.

- The next section (starting at measure 13) has the rehearsal letter "B" attached and is also labeled "**Pre-Chorus**." We have now changed to slash notation, where the chords are indicated without specific rhythms. In the second line of the "B" section we have the matching repeat sign for the one at the start of the "A" section, with the two measures before the repeat marked as a *first ending*. This means that, after playing through the "B" section and the first ending (measures 19–20), we repeat back to measure 5, then play the "A" and "B" sections again. This time we omit the first ending (measures 19–20) and skip directly from the end of measure 18 to measure 21 (the beginning of the *second ending*), then continue on to the "C" section.

- The next section (starting at measure 23) has the rehearsal letter "C" attached and is also labeled "**Chorus**." This section contains a mix of slash and rhythmic notation. At the end of measure 30 we notice a "coda" symbol (⊕). We ignore this sign for now, as we have not yet come to a "*D.S. al Coda*" or "*D.C. al Coda*" instruction. (Coda signs are not active until we have executed one of these instructions.) Then at the end of measure 34 we see a "*D.S. al Coda*" indication, which tells us to return to the sign (which is at the start of measure 5) and continue through the chart until we get to the (⊕) sign (at the end of measure 30). At this point we will jump to the "*Coda*" section [measure 35, preceded by the second (⊕) sign]. When taking the *D.S.*, the default assumption would be to observe the repeats (meaning that we would repeat the "A" and "B" sections again on the second pass through). But in this case the "*D.S. al Coda*" instruction also had the qualifier "*take 2nd ending*." This means that after the *D.S.*, we just play the "A" and "B" sections once and take the second ending (omitting the first ending by skipping from measure 18 to measure 21), before continuing to the "C" section.

- Once we are in the C section for the second time (after taking the *D.S.*), the (⊕) sign at the end of measure 30 becomes active. So after measure 30 we jump over to the "*Coda*" (measure 35), playing through to the end (measure 42). The end is sometimes labeled "*Fine*" (pronounced "FEE-nay"), which is Italian for "end."

Although this particular chart ("Roadmap Rock") has a **"D.S. al Coda"** instruction, you will often see **"D.C. al Coda"** used instead. **"D.C."** stands for *da capo*, meaning "from the top." So rather than returning to the 𝄋, you would go back to the beginning and continue from there.

You may also see the "Nashville numbering system" used on some charts as an alternative to the more traditional chord symbol notation. For example, to notate the chord progression of C–F–G in the key of C, the Nashville chart would simply show the numbers 1–4–5 above the staff. This can be a useful shorthand in the studio and can facilitate key changes more easily.

If you haven't done so already, consider investing in a computer notation program to run on your Mac or PC. This way you'll be able to produce publisher-quality charts and leadsheets of your songs. The leading notation software contenders in 2008 are Sibelius (www.sibelius.com) and Finale (www.codamusic.com). These programs are especially handy if your hand-copying skills (like mine) are less than world-class!

Advanced Stuff

CHAPTER 16
MORE CHORD EXTENSIONS AND ALTERATIONS

> **What's Ahead:**
> - Introduction to chord types
> - Extensions, alterations, and scale sources for all chord types
> - Using altered and extended chords

INTRODUCTION TO CHORD TYPES

In my classes and other books I make use of the term *chord type* as a way to group together chords with common characteristics. For example, we will see that the C major triad, C major seventh chord, and C major ninth chord all belong to the *major* chord type, as they all sound major and (for four-part and larger chords) all share the same definitive tones (which, as we saw in Chapter 12, are the third and seventh). So in this chapter we're going to extend each chord type beyond the ninth to include the eleventh and thirteenth. (You won't need to go any higher than the thirteenth of a chord—at least not in conventional Western music.) For each chord type, we'll also see what common forms are used and which scale contains all of the notes (basic chord tones and extensions).

> This chapter will develop the extensions, alterations, common forms, and scale sources for the following chord types:
> - major;
> - minor seventh;
> - minor seventh with flatted fifth;
> - minor sixth, minor/major seventh;
> - dominant seventh (with four levels of alterations);
> - diminished seventh.

EXTENSIONS, ALTERATIONS, AND SCALE SOURCES FOR ALL CHORD TYPES

THE MAJOR CHORD TYPE

In earlier chapters we derived the major triad (**Track 22**), major seventh chord (**Track 37**), and major ninth chord (**Track 53**). Now we'll extend the *major chord type* all the way up to the thirteenth.

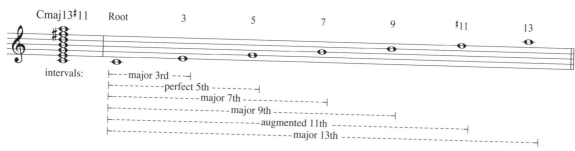

The chord symbol "Cmaj13#11" shown above the stack in the previous example is the version of this chord type that is created when all of the notes in the stack are used together. Note that the eleventh of this chord is in fact a sharped eleventh to avoid clashing with the third of the chord.

In general, use of the higher tones in the chord stack (and particularly the sharped eleventh here) is reserved for the more sophisticated and jazzy styles. Simpler pop or commercial styles will stick to the lower tones of the chord.

Next we'll look at the common forms of this major chord type: The chord symbols you will see typically used in songs, together with how these chords literally are spelled. Now a player or arranger is likely to voice these chords in different ways depending upon the musical style. For example, we've already seen some upper-structure voicings used on various chords; we'll develop these and other voicing concepts later in Chapter 19. For now, knowing how these chords are spelled will at least get you out of the gate, and knowing that they are all connected (i.e., members of the same chord type) is conceptually important. With this in mind, let's see all the common forms of this chord type, again built from the root C.

Track 62
(0:13)

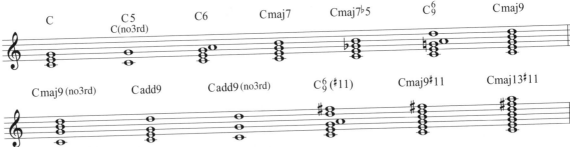

While most of these chords are definitive of the major chord type (containing the third and seventh/sixth of the chord), some are not—for example the Cmaj9(no3rd) or the Cadd9 chords. This is an important barometer of musical style: Mainstream jazz styles will generally use more definitive chords, while modern pop, rock, and smooth jazz will use less definitive and more "open" chords.

Now it's time to look at the scale source for this major chord type. This is derived by compressing all of the notes within the chord stack into a one-octave range (in this case, by taking the top notes D–F#–A and transposing them down one octave). It's important to realize that the scale source is simply a collective term, referring to all the notes (basic chord tones and extensions) that are available within the chord and is not necessarily indicative of the key that we're in at the time. Here's the scale source for the major chord type, built from C:

Track 62
(0:42)

The numbers below the staff show the functions of the scale degrees within this chord type. Notice that the "#11" and "♭5," and the "6" and "13," are *enharmonic equivalents* (which is a fancy way of saying that these different functions refer to the same tone). This scale is a C Lydian mode, which, as we saw in Chapter 6 (**Track 34**), is a G major scale displaced to start on the note C. Knowing the scale sources of chords is vital to improvising musicians, as they can use that scale as a source of notes when soloing over the chord changes.

Okay, now it's time to break out the stacks, common forms, and scale sources for all of the other chord types listed in the introduction, beginning with...

THE MINOR SEVENTH CHORD TYPE

In earlier chapters we derived the minor triad (**Track 23**), minor seventh chord (**Track 37**), and minor ninth chord (**Track 53**). Now we'll extend the minor seventh chord type all the way up to the thirteenth.

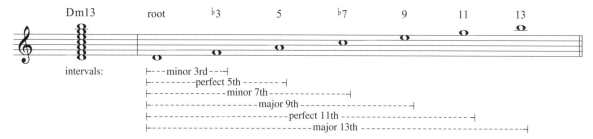

The chord symbol "Dm13" shown above the stack is the version of this chord type that is created when all of the notes in the stack are used together. Everything up to the eleventh on this chord type sounds stable and works for most styles. But the thirteenth sounds rather tense and is normally reserved for more sophisticated and modal jazz styles.

Next we'll look at the common forms of this minor seventh chord type, built from the root D.

Track 62
(0:12)

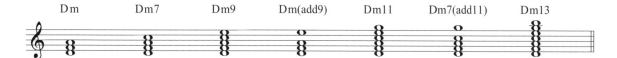

The minor triad is a less definitive form of this chord type, because it could also be a representative of the minor sixth or minor/major seventh chord type, as we will see shortly. Now we'll derive the scale source for the *minor seventh chord type*, again by compressing the chord stack into a one-octave range.

Track 62
(0:29)

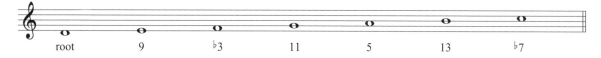

The chord functions of the scale degrees are shown below the staff. This scale is a D Dorian mode, which as we saw in Chapter 6 (**Track 33**) is a C major scale displaced to start on D.

THE MINOR SEVENTH WITH FLATTED FIFTH CHORD TYPE

In Chapter 7 we derived the minor seventh with flatted fifth chord (**Track 37**). Next we'll extend the minor seventh with flatted fifth chord type all the way up to the flatted thirteenth.

We can analyze the chords used in "Blue in Green" as follows:

Measures 1, 5, 11: The B♭maj9♯11 is a form of the major chord type (**Track 62**, twelfth chord).

Measures 2, 6, 12: The A7$^{♯9}_{♯5}$ is a form of the dominant seventh with sharped fifth/flatted thirteenth chord type (**Track 69**, third chord).

Measures 3, 10: The Dm9 is a form of the minor seventh chord type (**Track 63**, third chord).

Measure 3: The D♭7♯11 is a form of the dominant seventh with flatted fifth/sharped eleventh chord type (**Track 67**, fourth chord).

Measure 4: The Cm9 is a form of the minor seventh chord type (**Track 63**, third chord). The F13♭9 is a form of the dominant seventh with flatted ninth and sharped ninth chord type (**Track 68**, seventh chord).

Measures 7, 13: The Dm$^6_9$ is a form of the minor sixth, minor/major seventh chord type (**Track 65**, fifth chord).

Measure 8: The E7$^{♯9}_{♯5}$ is a form of the dominant seventh with sharped fifth/flatted thirteenth chord type (**Track 69**, third chord).

Measure 9: The Am9 is a form of the minor seventh chord type (**Track 63**, third chord).

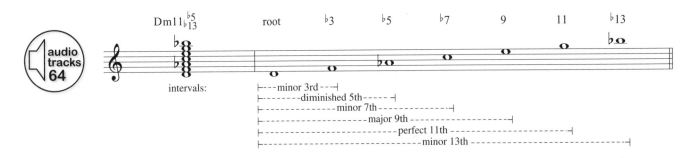

The chord symbol "Dm11$\flat^{\flat 5}_{13}$" shown above the stack is the version of this chord type that is created when all of the notes in the stack are used together. The use of this chord type (in any form) is indicative of a jazz or jazz-influenced style. The eleventh sounds stable, but the ninth and flatted thirteenth sound more tense and are normally reserved for more sophisticated jazz styles.

Next we'll look at the common forms of this chord type, built from the root D.

The diminished triad is a less definitive form of this chord type, because it could also be representative of the diminished seventh chord type, as we soon will see. Now we'll derive the scale source for this chord type:

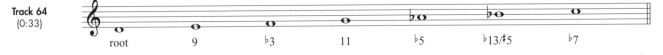

The chord functions of the scale degrees are shown below the staff, and we notice that the "$\flat 13$" and "$\sharp 5$" are enharmonic equivalents of this chord. This scale is the sixth mode of the F melodic minor scale (i.e., an F melodic minor scale displaced to start on its 6th degree). We heard the melodic minor scale earlier, on **Track 48**.

THE MINOR SIXTH, MINOR/MAJOR SEVENTH CHORD TYPE

In Chapter 7 we derived the minor sixth and minor/major seventh chords (**Track 37**). The *minor sixth, minor/major seventh chord type* includes both of these chords. Now we'll extend this chord type all the way up to the thirteenth.

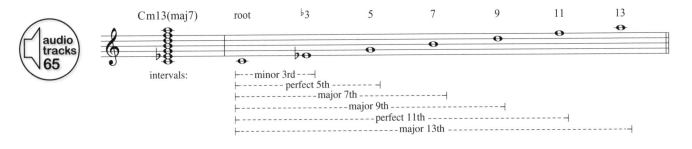

The chord symbol "Cm13(maj7)" shown above the stack in the previous example is the version of this chord type that is created when all of the notes in the stack are used together. The use of this chord type (in any form) is normally indicative of a jazz or jazz-influenced style. Adding the eleventh (especially in combination with the seventh) gives more tension to this chord.

Next we'll look at the common forms of this chord type, built from the root C.

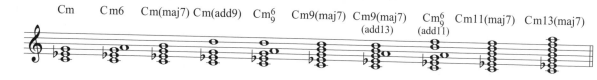

Track 65
(0:13)

The minor triad is a less definitive form of this chord type, because it could also be representative of the minor seventh chord type, as we saw earlier. Now we'll derive the scale source for this chord type:

Track 65
(0:35)

The chord functions of the scale degrees are shown below the staff. Notice that the "6" and "13" are the same note on this chord. (Normally, if the chord doesn't have a seventh then this note is referred to as a sixth, but if the chord does have a seventh then it's referred to as a thirteenth.) This scale is a C melodic minor scale, which we first heard on **Track 48**.

Following on from the discussion in Chapter 12, we can hear that the minor seventh and the minor sixth, minor/major seventh chord types give us substantially different flavors of minor chords. The minor seventh chord type will always sound more pop/commercial, whereas the minor sixth, minor/major seventh chord type is a signature jazz sound.

Sting (formerly of the Police) is a great example of an artist who uses the minor sixth, minor/major seventh chord type to give his pop/R&B songs a noticeable jazz flavor.

THE DOMINANT CHORD HIERARCHY

This section deals with dominant chords and their various alterations. This can be a confusing area for musicians and students, as there seems to be a large number of ways that alterations can be combined in dominant chords. So in my theory books and classes I have found it convenient to express the options for the extension and alteration of dominant chords in terms of a hierarchy, from least altered to most altered. Once you know where you are in this *dominant hierarchy*, you then know which chord tones are available, what the scale source is, and so on.

Before we get into the details, here's a quick summary of the different levels in the dominant chord hierarchy:

- Level One: unaltered dominant (including suspended dominant)
- Level Two: dominant chord with sharped eleventh/flatted fifth
- Level Three: dominant chord with flatted ninth and/or sharped ninth
- Level Four: dominant chord with sharped fifth/flatted thirteenth

The dominant hierarchy is cumulative, meaning that the higher levels will also include any alterations introduced at the lower levels.

- Level Three will also include the sharped eleventh/flatted fifth from Level Two.
- Level Four will also include the flatted ninth and sharped ninth from Level Three, and the sharped eleventh/flatted fifth from Level Two.

In jazz styles, it is routine for players and arrangers to upgrade basic dominant chord symbols by adding one or more alterations (context permitting). In terms of the structure presented here, this means advancing to a higher level in our dominant hierarchy.

Okay, now that we've covered some ground rules, let's explore the different levels individually.

LEVEL ONE: THE UNALTERED DOMINANT SEVENTH CHORD TYPE

Our first and simplest dominant chord has no alterations, but does come in both suspended and unsuspended forms. In Chapter 7 (**Track 37**) we learned the dominant seventh and suspended dominant seventh chords. The unaltered dominant seventh chord type includes both of these chords. Now we'll extend this chord type all the way up to the thirteenth.

Although the chord symbol "G13" is shown in the above example, this stack of notes has a conflict: The third (B) clashes with the fourth/eleventh (C), so these notes would not normally be used together. As we are about to see, the G13 chord uses the third instead of the fourth/eleventh, whereas the G13sus4 chord uses the fourth/eleventh (the suspension) instead of the third. This chord type is used widely (in unsuspended form) in basic jazz, blues, and gospel, and (in suspended form) in modern pop, R&B, and smooth jazz styles.

Next we'll look at the common forms of this chord type, built from the root G; these are divided into unsuspended (first system) and suspended (second system) forms.

Track 66
(0:13)

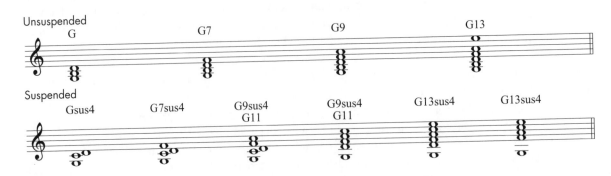

The major triad is a less-definitive form of the unsuspended dominant, and the suspended triad is a less-definitive form of the suspended dominant.

Among the suspended dominants, some alternate chords and chord symbols are shown.
- The chords symbols "G9sus4" and "G11" mean the same thing (as the eleventh is the suspension on the chord). Two possible placements of the fourth/eleventh are shown.
- Two alternate versions of the G13sus4 chord are shown (with and without the fifth, D). The fifth is not essential, as it does not impart any definition to the chord.

Any chord symbol consisting of just a letter name followed by a "7" or greater is a dominant chord symbol. G7, G9, and G13 are all unsuspended dominants and G11 is a suspended dominant (in which the fourth/eleventh has replaced the third).

Now we'll derive the scale source for this chord type by compressing the chord stack into a one-octave range.

Track 66
(0:36)

The chord functions of the scale degrees are shown below the staff. This scale is the G Mixolydian mode, which we met in Chapter 6 (**Track 33**)—a C major scale displaced to start on the G note.

LEVEL TWO: THE DOMINANT SEVENTH WITH FLATTED FIFTH/ SHARPED ELEVENTH CHORD TYPE

The next level in our hierarchy adds the flatted fifth/sharped eleventh to the dominant chord. In Chapter 7 (**Track 42**) we derived the dominant seventh with flatted fifth chord. Now we'll extend this chord type all the way up to the thirteenth.

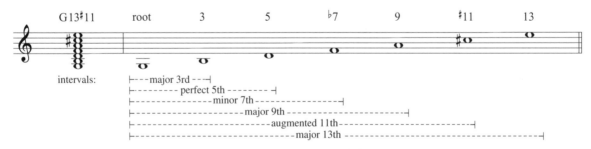

The chord symbol "G13♯11" shown above the stack is the version of this chord type that is created when all of the notes in the stack are used together. The use of this chord type (in any form) is normally indicative of a jazz or jazz-influenced style. This dominant chord is particularly suited for employment as a tritone substitute or dominant approach chord (see Chapter 13), with the sharped eleventh becoming the fifth of the subsequent chord.

Next we'll look at the common forms of this chord type, built from the root G.

Track 67
(0:13)

The major triad with flatted fifth is a less definitive form of this chord type. Now we'll derive the scale source for this chord type.

Track 67
(0:27)

The chord functions of the scale degrees are shown below the staff. Notice that the sharped eleventh and flatted fifth are enharmonic equivalents of this chord. This scale is the fourth mode of the D melodic minor scale (i.e., a D melodic minor scale displaced to start on its 4th degree). This scale is also referred to as the "Lydian dominant scale" by some jazz musicians and educators.

LEVEL THREE: THE DOMINANT SEVENTH WITH FLATTED NINTH AND SHARPED NINTH CHORD TYPE

The next level in our hierarchy adds the flatted ninth and sharped ninth to the dominant chord, while keeping the flatted fifth/sharped eleventh that was added at Level Two. In Chapter 11 we derived the dominant seventh with flatted ninth and dominant seventh with sharped ninth chords (**Track 54**). Now we'll extend this chord type all the way up to the thirteenth.

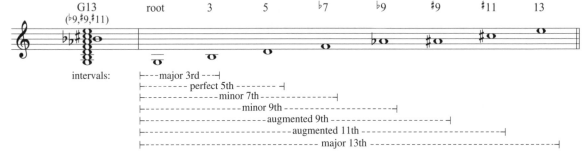

The chord symbol "G13(♭9, ♯9, ♯11)" shown above the stack is the version of this chord type that is created when all of the notes in the stack are used together. The use of this chord type (in any form) is normally indicative of a jazz or jazz-influenced style. Dominant chords at Level Three (or above) have a strong tendency to resolve to the next chord on a V–I basis, due to their altered ninth(s).

Next we'll look at the common forms of this chord type, built from the root G.

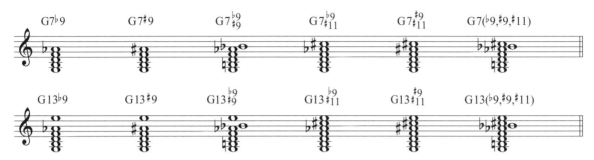

These common forms can be divided into two groups: Chords without the thirteenth (first line) and chords with the thirteenth (second line). Each chord in the second line is the result of adding a thirteenth to the corresponding chord in the first line. For example, if we take the first chord in the first line (G7♭9) and add a thirteenth, we get the first chord in the second line (G13♭9).

As you can see, all combinations of "♭9," "♯9," and "♯11" are possible within this chord type. In practice, however, the most-used combinations are:

- "♭9" as the only alteration (first line, first chord);
- "♭9" together with "♯11" (first line, fourth chord);
- "♭9" together with "13" (second line, first chord);
- "♭9" together with "♯11" and "13" (second line, fourth chord).

Now we'll derive the scale source for this chord type.

The chord functions of the scale degrees are shown below the staff. We notice that the sharped eleventh and flatted fifth are enharmonic equivalents of this chord. This scale has eight different pitches, in contrast to the seven-note scale sources we have seen so far. We only have seven letters in the musical alphabet, so we have to use one letter twice (in this case the sharped ninth is B♭, and the third is B♮). The interval between the first two notes (G–A♭) is a half step, and the interval between the next two notes (A♭–B♭) is a whole step. This interval pattern (half step–whole step) is then repeated as we continue up the scale. For this reason the scale is often referred to as the "half/whole" scale. We can also use the term *eight-note dominant* to describe this scale, as it is an eight-note dominant scale source. There's more about eight-note dominant scales in the next chapter.

LEVEL FOUR: THE DOMINANT SEVENTH WITH SHARPED FIFTH/ FLATTED THIRTEENTH CHORD TYPE

The final level in our hierarchy adds the sharped fifth/flatted thirteenth to the dominant chord, while retaining the flatted ninth and sharped ninth from Level Three and the flatted fifth/sharped eleventh from Level Two. In Chapter 7 we derived the dominant seventh with sharped fifth chord (**Track 42**). Also, in Chapter 11 we derived the dominant seventh with sharped fifth and flatted ninth chord and the dominant seventh with sharped fifth and sharped ninth chord (**Track 54**). Now we'll extend this chord type all the way up to the flatted thirteenth.

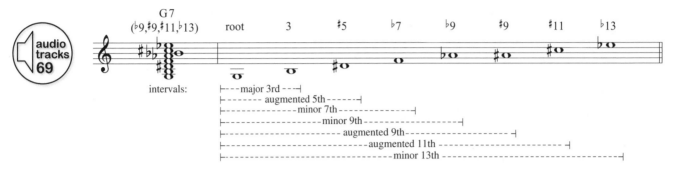

The chord symbol "G7(♭9, ♯9, ♯11, ♭13)" is the version of this chord type that is created when all of the notes in the stack are used together. At first sight it looks like we have eight different pitches (as in the Level Three dominant), but the "♯5" (D♯) and the "♭13" (E♭), which are both shown, are equivalent—so we're back to a seven-note scale for this chord, as we'll see in a moment. The use of this chord type (in any form) is normally indicative of a jazz or jazz-influenced style. Dominant chords at Level Four have a strong tendency to resolve to the next chord on a V–I basis, due to the altered thirteenth.

Sometimes you will see the suffix "7alt," as in the chord symbol "G7alt." This means that any/all of the Level Four alterations ("♭9," "♯9," "♯11," "♭13") are available for the chord.

Next we'll look at the common forms of this chord type, built from the root G.

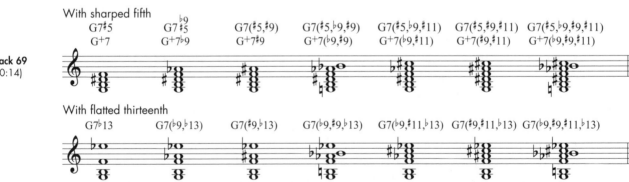

These common forms can be divided into two groups: Chords with the sharped fifth (first line) and chords with the flatted thirteenth (second line). We have seen that the sharped fifth is equivalent to the flatted thirteenth, so essentially these are different ways of writing the same chord. Also, we have two alternate symbols for each chord in the first line. The "+" sign in a chord symbol means "sharp the fifth of this chord," regardless of any other number actually following the "+" in the chord symbol. So for the first chord in the first line, we have two chord symbols: "G7♯5" (which means "G7 chord with sharped fifth") and "G+7" (which means "sharp the fifth of this G7 chord"). Below this, in the second line, we have the G7♭13 chord—which is also equivalent, as D♯ and E♭ are two names for the same pitch.

Track 69
(0:14)

As you can see, all combinations of "♭9," "♯9," "♭5/♯11," and "♯5/♭13" are possible within this chord type. In practice, however, the most-used combinations are:

- "♯5/♭13" as the only alteration (first chord of each line);
- "♯5/♭13" together with "♭9" (second chord of each line);
- "♯5/♭13" together with "♯9" (third chord of each line).

We'll now derive the scale source for this chord type.

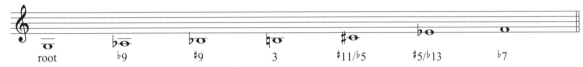

Track 69
(0:45)

The chord functions of the scale degrees are shown below the staff. Note that the sharped eleventh and flatted fifth, and the sharped fifth and flatted thirteenth, are enharmonic equivalents of this chord. This scale is the seventh mode of the A♭ melodic minor scale (i.e., an A♭ melodic minor scale displaced to start on its 7th degree). This scale is also referred to as the "altered scale" by some jazz musicians and educators.

Lastly, we'll explore a variant of the Level Four dominant chord that combines the "♯5/♭13" with the unaltered ninth. This has a more "floating," non-definitive quality and is useful in older pop and Broadway styles.

audio tracks 70

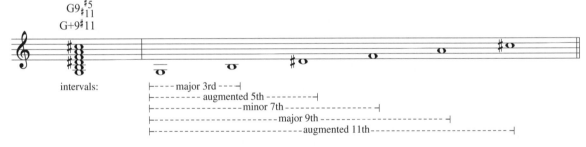

The alternate chord symbols "G9♯5♯11" and "G+9(♯11)" refer to the version of this chord type that is created when all of the notes in the stack are used together.

And now we'll derive the scale source for this variant.

Track 70
(0:11)

The chord functions of the scale degrees are shown below the staff. This scale has only six different pitches, so we will not need all seven letters of the musical alphabet (in this case, the letter E is not used). The interval between each successive pair of notes in this scale (G to A, A to B, and so on) is a whole step, so this scale is referred to as the *whole-tone scale*. We'll return to this scale in the next chapter.

THE DIMINISHED SEVENTH CHORD TYPE

In Chapter 7 we derived the diminished seventh chord (**Track 37**). Now we'll extend the *diminished seventh chord type* all the way up to the flatted thirteenth.

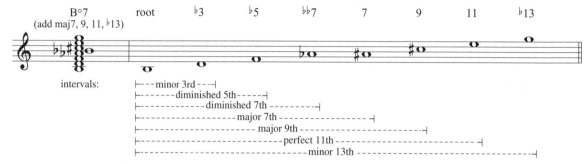

The chord symbol "B°7(add maj7, 9, 11, ♭13)" is the version of this chord type that is created when all of the notes in the stack are used together. The use of this chord type (with the upper extensions) is normally indicative of a jazz or jazz-influenced style. This chord type has several unique characteristics:

- The chord stack has two sevenths: The diminished seventh (A♭ in the above chord) is a definitive chord tone, while the major seventh (A♯ in the above chord) is an available upper extension.
- The chord stack can be divided into four basic chord tones (root, flatted third, flatted fifth, double flatted seventh) and four upper extensions (major seventh, ninth, eleventh, flatted thirteenth).
- Each of the upper extensions is equally important and the use of one does not imply the use of any other. For example, using "11" would not imply the presence of "maj7" or "9." For this reason, we can use "add" in the diminished chord symbol to refer to any/all of these extensions. For example, if we add the note C♯ to a B°7 chord, the recommended way to write this would be "B°7(add9)"; the symbol "B°9" would be incorrect.

In Chapter 13 (**Track 59**) we saw that the B°7 chord could substitute for the G7♭9 chord in a minor key. So we would expect a close relationship to exist between this diminished seventh chord type and the dominant seventh with flatted ninth and sharped ninth chord type discussed earlier. In fact, if you examine the chord stack for the G13(♭9, ♯9, ♯11) chord (**Track 68**), you'll discover that if we took the note G from the beginning and tacked it on at the end, we would get the sequence of notes for the B°7(add maj7, 9, 11, ♭13) chord stack (**Track 71**).

Now we'll look at the common forms of this chord type, built from the root B.

Track 71
(0:14)

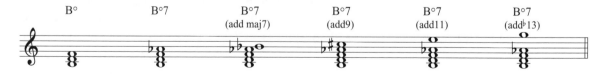

The diminished triad is a less definitive form of this chord type, as it could also be a version of the minor seventh with flatted fifth chord type that we saw earlier. The last four chords show each of the upper extensions added to the basic four-part diminished seventh chord. More advanced jazz applications will combine these extensions as needed.

Now we'll derive the scale source for this chord type.

Track 71
(0:28)

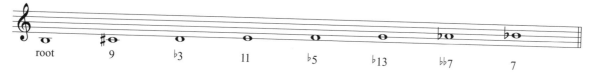

The chord functions of the scale degrees are shown below the staff. This scale has eight different pitches (like the dominant seventh with flatted ninth and sharped ninth chord type we saw earlier), so again we will need to use one letter of the musical alphabet twice (in this case, the major seventh is written as B♭, while the root is B♮). The interval between the first two notes (B–C♯) is a whole step and the interval between the next two notes (C♯–D) is a half step. This interval pattern (whole step–half step) is then repeated as we continue up the scale. For this reason the scale is often referred to as the "whole/half" scale. We can also use the term *eight-note diminished* to describe this scale, as it is an eight-note diminished scale source. There's more about eight-note diminished scales in the next chapter.

The affinity between this diminished seventh chord type and the dominant seventh with flatted ninth and sharped ninth chord type can also be seen by comparing their scale sources (which, as we'll discover in the next chapter, are the two varieties of octatonic scale). For now, note that if we take the eight-note dominant scale from **Track 68** and place the first three notes (G–A♭–B♭) at the end, we get the eight-note diminished scale from **Track 71**.

USING ALTERED AND EXTENDED CHORDS

To conclude this chapter, we'll see how some of these altered and extended chords are used in the classic jazz tune "Blue in Green," by Miles Davis. We'll also relate the chord symbols to the chord types previously outlined.

CHAPTER 17
MORE SCALES

What's Ahead:
- Whole-tone scale
- Octatonic scales

WHOLE-TONE SCALE

If we divide an octave into six equal parts, we get a series of whole steps, which are referred to collectively as a *whole-tone scale*. Here is a C whole-tone scale:

When writing out a whole-tone scale, we will use six (out of a possible seven) letters of the musical alphabet. Unlike with the major scales, there are some alternate naming options for notes within the whole-tone scale; for example, the F♯, G♯, and A♯ above could have been named G♭, A♭, and B♭.

This scale can in fact be named after any note in the scale; for example, this scale is also a D whole-tone scale, an E whole-tone scale, an F♯ whole-tone scale, and so forth. This is because the scale consists only of whole steps and can be started at any point. This interval structure also accounts for the rather "floating" impression left by this scale.

We can also find 3rds within the whole-tone scale by taking alternate notes of the scale. For example:

- we can start with C, then skip over D to E, creating the C–E major 3rd;
- we can start with D, then skip over E to F♯, creating the D–F♯ major 3rd;
- we can start with E, then skip over F♯ to G♯, creating the E–G♯ major 3rd;
- and so on....

Track 72
(0:07)

Like the whole-tone scale itself, these major 3rds also impart a "floating" impression, which can be put to good use in certain songs and styles. Following is the keyboard intro to the Stevie Wonder song "You Are the Sunshine of My Life." Check out the ascending major 3rds in measures 3–4 and 7–8.

You Are the Sunshine of My Life

Words and Music by
Stevie Wonder

These 3rds are from the F♯ whole-tone scale, which—as we have already discovered—contains the same notes as the C whole-tone scale. This type of sound is normally reserved for jazz or more impressionistic styles, but Stevie Wonder is known for smuggling jazz harmony and voicings into the pop charts!

Relating this example back to our work on chord types in Chapter 16: The F♯9♯5 chord is a variant of the Level Four dominant chord that contains the sharped fifth and unaltered ninth (refer to **Track 70**).

Our next example is what we call the "soap opera flashback." Running a whole-tone scale rapidly up and down (over two or more octaves) is a cliché phrase often used in old TV shows to indicate that a "flashback" in time is occurring. If you've heard this sound before… well, maybe you've been watching too much TV!

Track 72
(0:14)

OCTATONIC SCALES

Octatonic scales are eight-note scales that result from dividing an octave into four equal parts, and then further subdividing each part into half steps and whole steps. For example, if we take middle C up to the C an octave higher, then divide it into four equal parts, we get C–E♭–F♯–A–C (which spells a C diminished seventh chord). Each of the internal intervals is a minor 3rd (three half steps). If we then divide each of these minor 3rds into a half-step/whole-step pair, we get an *eight-note dominant scale*. Here is the C eight-note dominant scale:

In the previous example, note the "H" (half step) and "W" (whole step) characters below the staff. Because this scale starts with a half step and alternates between half and whole steps throughout, it is sometimes referred to as a "half/whole" scale.

We saw in Chapter 16 that this eight-note dominant scale was the source for the dominant seventh chord containing the flatted ninth, sharped ninth, and/or sharped eleventh (refer to **Track 68**). Now we'll find out what happens when we play the C eight-note dominant scale over a C7 chord.

Track 73
(0:08)

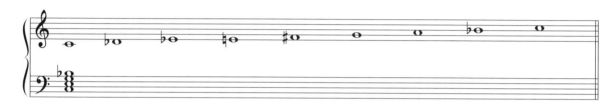

You can hear that some of the scale tones sound rather tense against the chord, as they are upper extensions or alterations on the C7 chord. These sounds are often found in jazz and Latin styles, but are rarely used in commercial pop and rock. Next up is a brief melody using the notes from the C eight-note dominant scale, again over a C7 chord.

Track 73
(0:17)

Now let's create a different octatonic scale. You'll remember that we divided the octave into four equal parts: C–E♭–F♯–A–C. Well, instead of dividing up each internal minor 3rd into a half-step/whole-step pair, let's now divide each interval into a whole-step/half-step pair. This creates an *eight-note diminished scale*. Here is the C eight-note diminished scale:

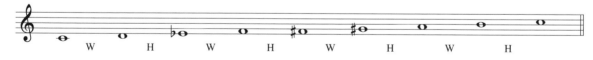

Note the "W" (whole step) and "H" (half step) characters below the staff. Because this scale starts with a whole step and alternates between whole and half steps throughout, it is sometimes referred to as a "whole/half" scale.

We saw in Chapter 16 that this eight-note diminished scale was the source for the diminished seventh chord (refer to **Track 71**). Now we'll find out what happens when we play the C eight-note diminished scale over a C°7 chord.

As before, some of the scale tones sound tense against the chord, as they are upper extensions of the C°7 chord. Here is a brief melody using the notes from the C eight-note diminished scale, again over a C°7 chord.

Something to watch out for: You will see different names for these scales in different books. For example, I have seen the eight-note dominant scale referred to as a "diminished scale" in some texts. You have been warned!

Experiment with your own whole-tone and octatonic scale melodies. Try writing down and/or recording the results. Let your ears be your guide…

CHAPTER 18
BEYOND DIATONIC CHORDS

What's Ahead:

- The secondary dominant concept
- The momentary key concept
- Mixing major and minor keys
- Non-harmonic tones

THE SECONDARY DOMINANT CONCEPT

In Chapter 12 we derived the II–V–I progressions in major and minor, and saw some examples of tunes using chords from different keys (i.e., beyond what was available in the key of the song). At that point we introduced the momentary key concept to keep track of where the song was going harmonically. Later in this chapter we'll do some more work with this idea.

First of all, though, we're going to explore a more traditional way of looking at chords borrowed from other keys, called the *secondary dominant concept*. This is an adequate alternative approach if the non-diatonic chord is a dominant chord (with a diatonic root) that leads back to a diatonic chord, normally on a circle-of-5ths (V–I) basis. We can apply this concept to the traditional song "Aura Lee."

Aura Lee

Words by W.W. Fosdick
Music by George R. Poulton

audio tracks 75

Using the secondary dominant concept, we can analyze the chords that are not diatonic to the main key of B♭ as follows:

Measures 2, 6, 14: The C7 chords lead into the F7 chords (in measures 3, 7, and 15) on a V–I basis. In other words, if we were in the key of F, the C7 would be the V chord leading back to the tonic. The C7 is therefore a secondary dominant and can be called V of V (as it is a V chord with respect to the F7 chord, which in turn is a V chord in the key of the song).

Measure 9: The D7 chord leads into the Gm chord in measure 10 on a V–I basis. D7 is therefore a secondary dominant and can be called V of VI (as it is a V chord with respect to the Gm chord, which in turn is a VI chord in the key of the song).

Measure 10: The B♭7 chord leads into the E♭maj7 chord in measure 11 on a V–I basis. The B♭7 is therefore a secondary dominant and can be called V of IV (as it is a V chord with respect to the E♭maj7 chord, which in turn is a IV chord in the key of the song).

Measure 13: The G7 chord leads into the C7 chord in measure 14 on a V–I basis. The G7 is therefore a secondary dominant and can be called V of II (as it is a V chord with respect to the C7 chord, which is built from the 2nd degree of the key of the song and acts as a secondary dominant of the F7 discussed above).

Next up is the chorus from the John Lennon ballad "Imagine," which uses secondary dominant chords in a different way. This example includes the piano accompaniment figure, written below the vocal staff.

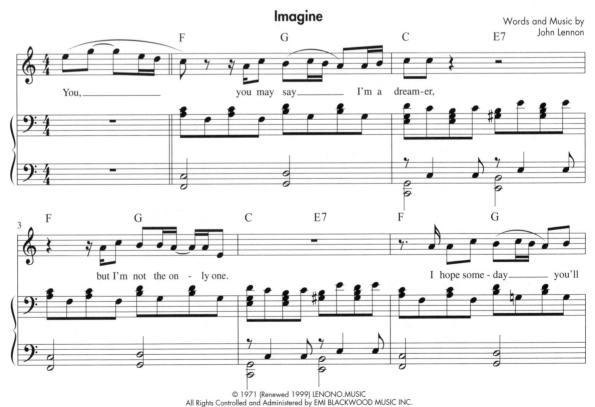

The only chords here that are not diatonic to the key of C are the E7 dominant chords. Using the secondary dominant concept, we could call the E7 chord a V of VI (Am being the VI chord in the key of C). However, this example is different in that the E7 chord isn't actually followed by an Am chord; instead it moves to an F major chord (a IV chord in the key of the song). This is not as typical, but it still works because the E7 chord leads smoothly into the F major chord by a half step.

THE MOMENTARY KEY CONCEPT

When analyzing tunes that employ multiple II–V or II–V–I progressions (which may include substitute chords) from different keys, the more traditional secondary dominant approach becomes inadequate. It is recommended that you instead use the *momentary key* concept. We got a head start on this back in Chapters 12–13, when we began to analyze the II–V–I progression and substitute chords as used in jazz standards. Now it's time to delve into this in more detail, by developing a three-stage procedure that we can use to analyze tunes using this II–V–I-style harmony (this includes jazz standards and older pop styles like that of the Beatles).

Stage 1: Look for the dominant chords first. The default assumption is that they will be V chords in either the key of the song or another momentary key. If the dominant is not functioning as a V, then the two most likely options are:
- it is a dominant approach chord (refer to **Track 60**), moving down by half step to the next chord;
- it is a ♭VII dominant, moving up to the tonic chord by a whole step (for example, F7–Gmaj7), which is a signature jazz sound.

Stage 2: Look before the dominant for a II chord (or its substitute) and after the dominant for a I chord (or its substitute). Also, don't forget that we can mix II–V–I progressions (including substitute chords) from major and minor keys (for example, Dm7–G7♭9–Cmaj7 is a mixed II–V–I progression, with the II and I chords coming from the key of C major and the V chord coming from the key of C minor). Review Chapters 12–13 if you're still not sure about this. And don't forget that we can do a VII-for-V substitution on the dominant chord itself—although this doesn't happen a lot in actual practice, and when it does happen it's normally in minor keys.

Stage 3: Any chords still to be analyzed after Stages 1–2 are likely to be:
- diatonic chords in the key of the song;
- substitute chords in the preceding and/or following momentary key;
- momentary I chords in a new key.

Next we'll look at the Beatles ballad "Here, There and Everywhere," checking out the momentary keys being used in the harmony.

Here, There and Everywhere

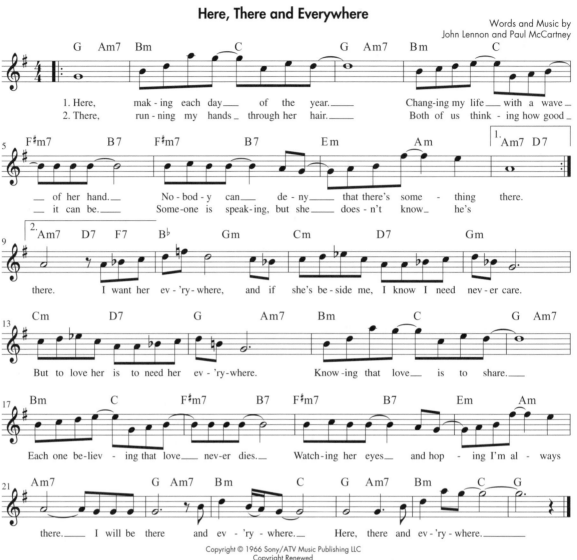

Words and Music by
John Lennon and Paul McCartney

Although most of the chords in this song are diatonic to the key of G major, there are some other momentary keys used as follows:

Measures 5–6, 18–19: The B7 chord is preceded by an F♯m7 chord. The two together create a II–V progression in E major. Note that the Em following the B7 chords is both a momentary I in E minor (creating a mixed II–V–I), and a VI in the key of the song (G major). The Em is therefore a linking chord between these keys.

Measure 9–12: The F7 chord is followed by a B♭ major chord, creating a V–I progression in B♭ major. This is then followed by the VI and II chords in the same momentary key. The D7 is from the key of the song, but it leads to a I in G minor (a mixed V–I progression).

Now it's time to look at a jazz tune with a more sophisticated mix of momentary keys and substitute chords. Following is the leadsheet for the standard "I Remember You" by Victor Schertzinger.

I Remember You
from the Paramount Picture THE FLEET'S IN

Words by Johnny Mercer
Music by Victor Schertzinger

Although this song is in the key of G major, there are lots of other momentary keys and substitute chords used as follows:

Measures 2, 10, 26: The F#7 chord is preceded by a C#m7 chord, a II–V progression in B major. In each case, however, the F#7 chord moves back to Gmaj7, which is the overall tonic. This works because the F#7 chord leads smoothly, by a half step, to Gmaj7.

Measures 4–5, 12–13,16–17: The G7sus4 and G7 chords are each preceded by a Dm7 chord and followed by a Cmaj7 chord, creating II–V–I progressions in C major.

Measures 6–7, 14–15: The F7 chord is preceded by a Cm7 chord, a II–V progression in B♭ major. The F7 resolves to the I in measure 7, but leads back to Gmaj7 in measure 15. Here F7 is functioning as a ♭VII dominant, moving up to Gmaj7 (the tonic chord in the key of the song) by a whole step.

Measures 18–19, 20–21: The B7♭9 chord is preceded by an F#m7 chord and followed by an Emaj7 chord; this constitutes a mixed II–V–I progression in E major/minor. The C#m7 in measure 19 is a VI chord in the momentary key of E major.

Measures 22–23:	The A7 chord is preceded by an Em7 chord and followed by a Dmaj7 chord, a II–V–I progression in D major. The Bm7 in measure 23 is a VI chord in the same momentary key.
Measures 28–29:	The E7♭9 chord is preceded by a Bm7 chord and followed by an Am7 chord, a mixed II–V–I progression in A major/minor.
Measure 30:	The F9 chord functions as a ♭VII dominant, moving up to Gmaj7 by a whole step.
Measures 32–33:	Here we a have a disguised II–V–I progression, where a tritone substitution has been applied to the V chord. (The chords moving by descending half steps C♯–C♮–B are an important clue here.) C9 is a tritone substitute for F♯7♯9, which would have created a II–V–I progression in B minor.
Measures 33–34:	Measure 33's Bm7 becomes a II chord in another disguised II–V–I progression. B♭7 is a tritone substitute for E7, which would have created a mixed II–V–I progression in A major/minor.
Measures 34–35:	Measure 34's Am7 becomes a II chord in a mixed II–V–I progression back to G, with the D7♭9 chord being a V in G minor.

"I Remember You" is an enduringly popular jazz standard. Originally published in 1941, it was featured in the movie *The Fleet's In*, starring Dorothy Lamour and William Holden. The diverse list of pop and jazz artists who have covered the song includes the Beatles, Tony Bennett, Stan Getz, Ella Fitzgerald, Björk, Art Garfunkel, John Denver, George Michael, and Diana Krall.

MIXING MAJOR AND MINOR KEYS

We've already seen examples of mixed II–V–I progressions: For example, taking a II chord from C major (Dm7), a V chord from C minor (G7♭9), and a I chord from C major (Cmaj7). This is commonly done in jazz and jazz-influenced styles. Now we'll look at the equivalent idea in modern pop/rock/R&B styles, which is to mix diatonic triads from a major scale and a minor scale (normally the natural minor) built from the same tonic. Some educators and texts refer to this concept as *modal mixture*. Before looking at the next song, let's review the triads available within the C major and C natural minor scales.

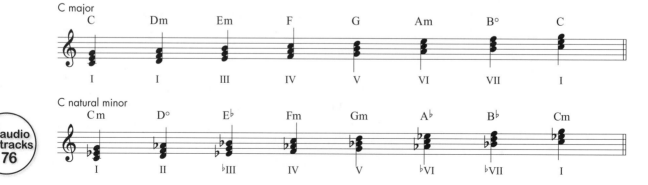

A lot of hit songs have been written using this mix of triads! We can hear this concept at work in the song "Crazy Little Thing Called Love" from the rock band Queen.

Crazy Little Thing Called Love

Words and Music by
Freddie Mercury

Oh, this thing___ called love, well I just___ can't__ han - dle it.___ This thing_

___ called love, I__ must___ get a - round to it.___ I ain't___

read - y. Cra - zy lit - tle thing called love.

Although this song is written in the key of C and includes diatonic triads from C major (i.e., the C and F major triads), it also includes triads from the C natural minor scale as follows:

Measure 4, 8, 10:   The B♭ major chord is the ♭VII triad from the C natural minor scale.

Measure 10:   The A♭ major chord is the ♭VI triad from the C natural minor scale.

Queen's lead singer Freddie Mercury reportedly wrote "Crazy Little Thing Called Love" in under ten minutes. The song's rockabilly style and Elvis Presley-influenced vocals contrasted with the grandiose rock epics that Queen was otherwise known for. Its catchy melody and upbeat lyric has made it one of Queen's best-loved songs, and it became the band's first #1 hit single in the US.

Photo by Simon Fowler/© Elektra Records/Photofest

Queen

The last example combined chords from major and minor scales built from the same tonic. Now we will look at two pieces that combine chords from the major and relative minor scales. You'll remember from Chapter 9 that the relative minor begins on the 6th degree of the corresponding major scale. For example, the keys of G major and E minor are relative to one another and share the same key signature (one sharp). As the E natural minor scale has the same notes as the G major scale, deriving triads from the E natural minor scale would give us the same triads available in G major. However, deriving triads from the E melodic or harmonic minor scales would give us some extra triad options—in particular the major V triad in the minor key (i.e., a B major triad in the key of E minor). So before we look at the next piece, let's review the triads that are available within the G major and E harmonic minor scales.

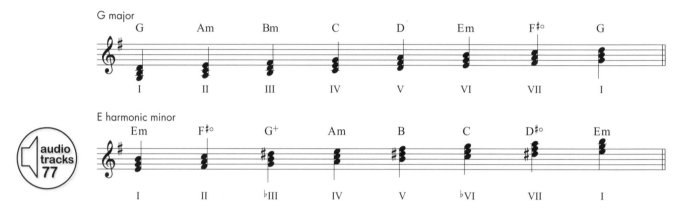

Now here is an excerpt from *In Church* by Tchaikovsky, which moves between the relative keys of G major and E minor, using a mix of the above triads.

In Church (A L'eglise), Op. 39, No. 24
from ALBUM POUR ENFANTS (ALBUM FOR CHILDREN)

By Pyotr Il'yich Tchaikovsky

We can analyze the triad progression and movement between the major and relative minor keys as follows:

Measures 1–2: The piece begins in the relative minor key (E minor), moving from the E minor triad (I) to the B major triad (V) and back again. The E minor triad belongs to both the G major scale and the E harmonic minor scale, and in this piece it acts as a linking chord between the major and relative minor keys.

Measures 3–7: The E minor chord in measure 2 leads us into the key of G major in these measures, where we find the following chords: D major (V), E minor (VI), D major (V), G major (I), D major (V), and E minor (VI). This last E minor triad leads us back into the relative minor key again.

Measures 8–9: Now we're back in the key of E minor with a B major (V) triad leading to the E minor triad (I) in measure 9. This E minor triad then leads us back to the key of G major again, being followed by a D major triad (V in G).

Measures 10–12: After the G major triad (I in G), we then transition back to the key of E minor (ending with the V–I triad progression). This section also uses some slash chords: the F#° triad inverted over its third (A), and the Em triad inverted over its fifth (B).

On to our next example that combines chords from the major and relative minor keys: The Beatles ballad "Yesterday," written by Paul McCartney. This song uses some four-part chords and II–V–I-type harmonies, so we can look at the movement between major and minor keys from a momentary-key point of view (similar to how we looked at the Beatles song "Here, There and Everywhere" earlier in the chapter). This song is in the key of F major, so we'll be on the lookout for movement between the relative keys of F major and D minor.

Yesterday

Words and Music by
John Lennon and Paul McCartney

Although most of the chords used in this song are diatonic to F major (including various II–V–I, IV–V–I, and IV–I progressions), the song does go through some other momentary keys (in particular the relative minor) as follows:

Measures 2–3, 9–10, 24–25: The Em7–A7–Dm is a mixed II–V–I progression ending in D minor (the relative minor). Note the accidentals in the melody (B♮ and C♯) in measure 2—the melody at this point is using a D melodic minor scale.

Measures 6, 13, 28: The Dm7–G7 is a II–V progression in C major.

Measures 15–16, 19–20: The Em7–A7–Dm in the bridge is another mixed II–V–I progression ending in D minor.

NON-HARMONIC TONES

Finally, we'll explore the use of *non-harmonic tones* in some well-known pieces. A *non-harmonic tone* is a melody note that appears to contradict the harmony in force at the time. This may work for several reasons: The melodic motif may be sufficiently strong to counteract any vertical contradictions that occur, and/or the non-harmonic tone may resolve strongly back into the harmony again (typically by a half step). The melody may also have a distinctive rhythm pattern (for example, using anticipations) which then floats over (and is not constrained by) the harmonic structure of the song.

Our first example in this section uses suspensions in the melody. We saw in Chapter 5 that a suspended chord is one where the third has been replaced by another note (most typically the fourth). If we use the fourth in the melody on a major chord, this would be a non-harmonic tone which would then normally resolve to the third. This occurs twice in the jazz standard "Stella by Starlight" by Victor Young.

Stella by Starlight
from the Paramount Picture THE UNINVITED

Words by Ned Washington
Music by Victor Young

Notice in measures 9 and 13 that we have the fourth in the melody over a major chord: The E♭ over the B♭maj7 chord in measure 9, and the B♭ over the Fmaj7 chord in measure 13. These are non-harmonic tones that resolve to the third of each major chord on beat 2 of these measures. These resolutions, together with the strength of the melody as a whole, allow the ear to accept these non-harmonic tones.

Next we'll look at two examples that use chromatic neighbor tones. These non-harmonic tones are *chromatic* (i.e., do not belong within) to the key of the piece, are normally placed on a weak beat (or an upbeat), and almost always resolve into an adjacent diatonic tone by a half step. Heading back into the classical world, we'll see this concept at work in Beethoven's famous *Minuet in G Major*.

Minuet in G Major

By Ludwig van Beethoven

In measure 1, notice the A♯ and C♯ on the last sixteenth note of each beat in the treble-clef part. These are chromatic neighbor tones, which lead back to the diatonic tones B and D. A similar idea occurs in measure 5, with the chromatic tone A♯ again leading into the diatonic tone B (the F♯–G movement below is diatonic).

Next up is a simple piano arrangement of the traditional song "Down by the Riverside," which uses chromatic neighbor tones in a similar way.

Down by the Riverside

African American Spiritual

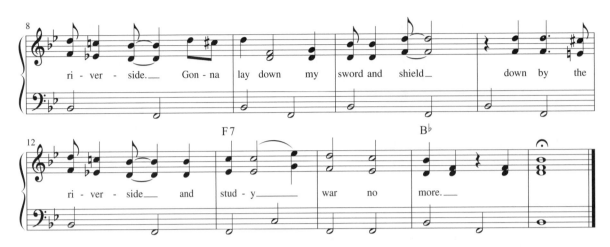

In measure 3, notice the C♯ and E halfway through beat 4 in the treble-clef part. These are chromatic neighbor tones, which lead back to the diatonic tones D and F (within the B♭ major chord) in the next measure. The same idea is repeated in measures 7 and 11. And in measure 5 the chromatic neighbor tones G♯ and B♮ resolve to A and C (within the F7 chord) in measure 6.

To conclude this chapter, we'll look at the verse melody in Nirvana's grunge anthem "Smells Like Teen Spirit." This is an interesting example of repeated melodic *anticipations*, giving the melody something of a separate life from the harmonic structure of the song. This allows the melody (which includes some mild non-harmonic tones) to float over the chord changes.

Smells Like Teen Spirit

Words and Music by Kurt Cobain, Krist Novoselic and Dave Grohl

Notice how the melody is almost always *anticipating* (i.e., landing an eighth note ahead of) beats 1 and 3 in each measure. Although there are no notes that are chromatic to the key, there are some melody notes that are non-harmonic tones: For example, the E♭ on the B♭5 chords. The open sound of these root–fifth chords, together with the rhythmic anticipations and the character of the melody, helped make this song one of the all-time rock classics of the 1990s!

CHAPTER 19

UPPER-STRUCTURE VOICINGS AND SHAPES

> ***What's Ahead:***
> - Upper-structure triads and slash chords
> - Four-part upper-structure chords and slash chords
> - Double-4th and "7–3" extended voicings
> - Polychord voicings

UPPER-STRUCTURE TRIADS AND SLASH CHORDS

Contemporary styles often require the use of *upper-structure* voicings. These are three- or four-part chords that are built from a chord tone (third, fifth, seventh, etc.) of the overall chord. This is a very efficient voicing method, not least because the same upper structure can be used within various different overall chords. First we will look at the use of upper-structure triads, sometimes referred to as triad-over-root voicings. Different rules will apply depending upon what overall type of chord (major, minor, dominant, etc.) we are trying to create. Here are the commonly used triad-over-root voicings for major chords:

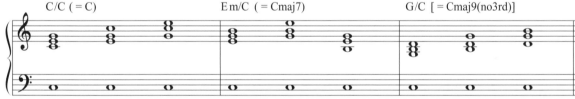

The upper structures in the treble-clef part (triads in this case) are each built from different chord tones of the overall chord (from the root, third, or fifth of C major in this case). Each inversion of the upper structure is shown in the treble clef, while the root of the overall chord is shown in the bass clef. There are two chord symbols above each measure. The first is a slash chord symbol with the upper-structure triad to the left of the slash, and the root to the right. The second is the equivalent composite symbol, showing the overall chord created by placing the upper structure over the root. The specific voicings shown can be analyzed as follows:

- In the first measure, we are building a major triad from the root of the overall major chord (C/C). This is a simple triad-over-root voicing and just creates a basic major chord.
- In the second measure, we are building a minor triad from the third of the overall major chord (Em/C). This creates a major seventh chord overall.
- In the third measure, we are building a major triad from the fifth of the overall major chord (G/C). This creates a major ninth chord with an omitted third.

Next we'll check out the commonly used triad-over-root voicings for minor and suspended dominant chords.

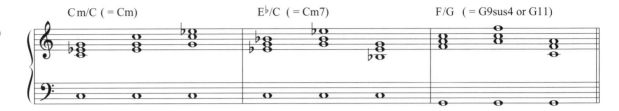

These voicings can be analyzed as follows:

- In the first measure, we are building a minor triad from the root of the overall minor chord (Cm/C). This is a simple triad-over-root voicing and just creates a basic minor chord.
- In the second measure, we are building a major triad from the third of the overall minor chord (E♭/C). This creates a minor seventh chord overall. (Note that E♭ is a minor 3rd above the root of C.)
- In the third measure, we are building a major triad from the seventh of the overall suspended dominant chord (F/G). This creates a suspended dominant ninth (a.k.a. dominant eleventh) chord. (Note that F is a minor 7th above the root of G.) This voicing can also work as a less-defined incomplete minor eleventh chord.

And now we'll look at some triad-over-root voicings for inverted major and minor chords, placed over the third or fifth in the bass.

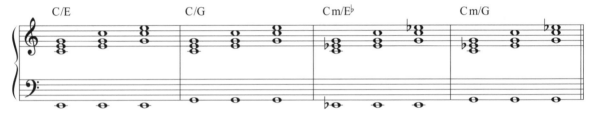

Note that the term *inverted* here refers to these triads being placed over the third or fifth in the bass (not the fact that the upper triads themselves may be inverted). These voicings can be analyzed as follows:

- In the first measure, the major triad is placed over its third in the bass (C/E).
- In the second measure, the major triad is placed over its fifth in the bass (C/G).
- In the third measure, the minor triad is placed over its third in the bass (Cm/E♭).
- In the fourth measure, the minor triad is placed over its fifth in the bass (Cm/G).

These are all common sounds in contemporary pop, rock, and R&B styles. Next up is a brief chord progression in a pop/rock rhythmic style, using some of these triad-over-root voicings.

We can summarize the voicing choices in the previous example as follows:

- In the first measure, the Cmaj7 chord is voiced by building a minor triad from the third (Em/C).
- In the second measure (beat 1), the Dm7 chord is voiced by building a major triad from the third (F/D).
- In the second measure (beat 3), the G11 chord is voiced by building a major triad from the seventh (F/G).

In the previous example all the upper-structure triads are in second inversion, resulting in smooth voice leading through the progression. Note that we showed only the composite chord symbols (Cmaj7, Dm7, G11) above the staff, which is the most typical situation when reading from a chart. However, we can translate these into slash chord symbols to derive the necessary triad-over-root voicings.

Although you will see the composite chord symbols on charts most of the time, you will still commonly see slash chord symbols for inverted major and minor chords (as on **Track 80**), and also when a series of triads is played over a repeated bass note, or *pedal point*.

Now it's time to look at some well-known music that uses triad-over-root harmony. Perhaps one of the most famous examples is the 1980s rock hit "Jump" from Van Halen. The synthesizer intro to this song uses several triad-over-root chords, mostly over a repeated bass note of C.

Jump

Words and Music by David Lee Roth,
Edward Van Halen, Alex Van Halen and Michael Anthony

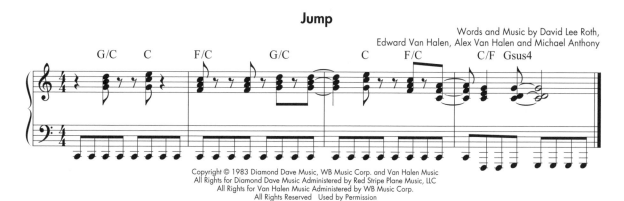

We can analyze the triad-over-root chord symbols and voicings in "Jump" as follows:

Measures 1, 2: The G/C chord is voiced by building a major triad from the fifth of a C major chord.

Measures 1, 3: The C chord is simply voiced by building a major triad from the root of a C major chord.

Measures 2, 3: The F/C chord is voiced by inverting an F major triad with its fifth (C) in the bass.

Measure 4: The C/F chord is voiced by building a major triad from the fifth of an F major chord, and the Gsus4 chord is voiced by suspending the G major triad, replacing the third (B) with the fourth (C).

Next up is an excerpt from Chopin's *Prelude in C Minor*, which was also used as the intro to "Could It Be Magic" by Barry Manilow. This uses an interesting mix of triad-over-root and four-part chords.

Prelude in C Minor, Op. 28, No. 20

By Fryderyk Chopin

Again, we wouldn't normally write chord symbols on a piece of classical music! However, the symbols help us see that the chords in this piece fall into the following categories:

- triad-over-root chords;
- four-part dominant seventh chords: G7, C7, D7 (see Chapter 7);
- larger dominant chords with upper extensions/alterations: G7#5, Eb13, D13, Ab7#11 (see Chapter 16);
- four-part minor seventh chords using "7–3" voicings: Bm7 and Am7 (see Chapter 12);
- minor add9 chords: Fm(add9) (see Chapter 11).

We can analyze the triad-over-root chord symbols and voicings as follows:

Measures 1, 3, 5, 7, 8: The Cm chord is voiced simply by building a minor triad from the root (Cm/C).

Measure 1: The Fm7 chord is voiced by building a major triad from the third (Ab/F).

Measures 2, 8: The Ab and Db chords are voiced simply by building major triads from the roots (Ab/Ab, Db/Db).

Measures 4, 6: The G chord is voiced simply by building a major triad from the root (G/G).

Measure 5: The Ab/C chord is voiced by inverting an Ab major triad over its third (C) in the bass. The Gm/Bb chord is voiced by inverting a G minor triad over its third (Bb) in the bass.

Measure 6: The G/F implies a four-part G7 chord over its seventh in the bass. (This is often used as part of a descending bass line.)

Measure 7: The Cm/Eb chord is voiced by inverting a C minor triad over its third (Eb) in the bass. The G/B chord is voiced by inverting a G major triad over its third (B) in the bass.

FOUR-PART UPPER-STRUCTURE CHORDS AND SLASH CHORDS

Now it's time to look at some *four-part upper-structure voicings*. These are four-part chords that are built from a chord tone (third, fifth, seventh, etc.) of the overall chord. Here are the commonly used four-part, chord-over-root voicings for major and minor chords:

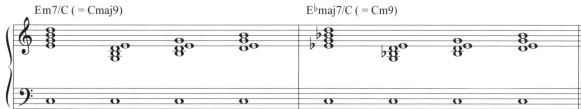

Note that (as with the triad-over-root voicings) both slash chord and composite chord symbols are shown, and all inversions of the upper structures are shown. The specific voicings can be analyzed as follows:

- In the first measure, we are building a minor seventh four-part chord from the third of the overall major chord (Em7/C). This creates a major ninth chord.
- In the second measure, we are building a major seventh four-part chord from the third of the overall minor chord (Ebmaj7/C). This creates a minor ninth chord. (Note that Eb is a minor 3rd above the root of C.)

Next we will look at a series of four-part, chord-over-root voicings for dominant and suspended dominant chords. These are all common sounds in R&B and jazz styles.

Track 82
(0:19)

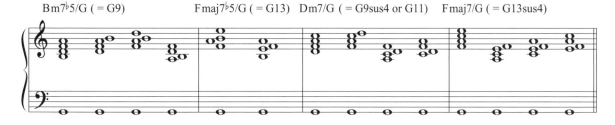

These voicings can be analyzed as follows:
- In the first measure, we are building a minor seventh with flatted fifth four-part chord from the third of the overall dominant chord (Bm7b5/G). This creates a dominant ninth chord.

- In the second measure, we are building a major seventh with flatted fifth four-part chord from the seventh of the overall dominant chord (Fmaj7♭5/G). This creates a dominant thirteenth chord.
- In the third measure, we are building a minor seventh four-part chord from the fifth of the overall suspended dominant chord (Dm7/G). This creates a suspended dominant ninth (or dominant eleventh) chord.
- In the fourth measure, we are building a major seventh four-part chord from the seventh of the overall suspended dominant chord (Fmaj7/G). This creates a suspended dominant thirteenth chord.

Next up is a brief chord progression in an R&B/smooth jazz rhythmic style, using some of these voicings. This example shows just the composite chord symbols, which we can then translate into slash chord symbols to derive the necessary four-part, chord-over-root voicings.

Track 82
(0:53)

nuts
& bolts

We can summarize the voicing choices in this example as follows:
- In the first measure, the Cmaj9 chord is voiced by building a minor seventh four-part chord from the third (Em7/C).
- In the second measure (beat 1), the Fmaj9 chord is voiced by building a minor seventh four-part chord from the third (Am7/F).
- In the second measure (beat 3), the G13sus4 chord is voiced by building a major seventh four-part chord from the seventh (Fmaj7/G).

Now we'll see some of these voicings used in the keyboard figure from the popular Doobie Brothers song "What a Fool Believes," written by Michael McDonald and Kenny Loggins.

What a Fool Believes

Words and Music by
Michael McDonald and Kenny Loggins

The chords in this example contain a mix of four-part, chord-over-root voicings and triad-over-root voicings. This use is typical in more advanced contemporary pop/R&B styles.

Measure 1: The A♭13sus chord is voiced by building a major seventh four-part chord from the seventh (G♭maj7/A♭), leading to the A♭9 chord, which is voiced by building a minor seventh with flatted fifth four-part chord from the third (Cm7♭5/A♭). The G♭add9 chord is voiced with the ninth, third, and fifth of the chord (sometimes referred to as a *cluster*). This leads to an upper A♭ triad shape that momentarily implies an A♭7 chord, with its seventh (G♭) in the bass.

Measures 1–2: The D♭/F chord is voiced by placing a D♭ major triad over its third (F) in the bass. The remaining upper shapes in measure 2 are heard in the context of this D♭ major chord: The A♭ major triads are built from the fifth, and the three-note cluster (repeated from measure 1) is now the fifth, sixth, and root of the chord.

Measure 3: The E♭m7 chord is voiced by building a major triad from the third (G♭/E♭). (The C° upper *passing triad* is derived from the E♭ Dorian mode). The A♭9sus4 chord is voiced by building a major triad from the seventh (G♭/A♭). The A°7 chord is voiced simply by building a diminished seventh chord from the root (A°7/A). The B♭m7 chord is voiced simply by building a minor seventh chord from the root (B♭m7/B♭).

Measure 4: The upper shapes during beats 1 and 2 are heard in the context of the preceding B♭m7 chord: The D♭ major triad is built from the third, and the A♭ major triad is built from the seventh. The A9 chord is voiced with the seventh, ninth, and third of the chord (another cluster voicing). This leads to an upper C minor triad shape, momentarily implying an Am7♭5 chord at the end of the measure.

origins

"What a Fool Believes" was recorded for the 1978 Doobie Brothers album, *Minute by Minute*, and featured Michael McDonald's inimitable lead vocal style. As a single, the song briefly topped the charts in the US and received two Grammy awards in 1980. Co-writer Kenny Loggins also included a version of the song on his 1978 album, *Nightwatch*. The song has been covered by numerous artists including Aretha Franklin, George Michael, Dionne Warwick, and Matt Bianco.

Photo by Warner Bros. Records/Photofest
The Doobie Brothers

DOUBLE-4TH AND "7–3" EXTENDED VOICINGS

In this section we'll look at some more advanced chord voicings (suitable for more sophisticated pop/R&B as well as jazz styles), beginning with *double-4th shapes*. These are three-note voicings created by stacking two perfect 4ths on top of another. In my books and classes I use the term "shape" when referring to these, because (unlike the upper-structure triad and four-part voicings) they are not easily or helpfully described with individual chord symbols. Now we'll see how to use this shape to create double-4th-over-root voicings for major, minor, and suspended dominant chords.

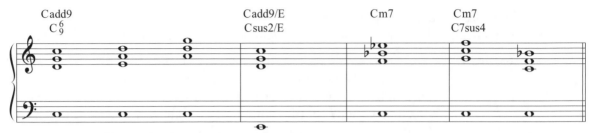

Although this example shows the double-4th shapes in root position, note that (as with the triad and four-part upper structures) they are often inverted. The specific voicings shown can be analyzed as follows:

- In measure 1, we are building double-4th shapes from the ninth, third, and sixth of the overall C major chord. These upper shapes add various combinations of the sixths and ninths to the chord.
- In measure 2, a double-4th shape built from the ninth of the C major chord has been placed over the third (E) in the bass.
- In measure 3, we are building a double-4th shape from the fourth/eleventh of the overall Cm7 chord. This upper shape adds the fourth/eleventh to the chord.
- In measure 4, we are building double-4th shapes from the fifth and root of the overall C minor or C suspended dominant chord (these combinations work for both types of chord). Both of these upper shapes add the fourth/eleventh to the minor chord.

Although we used detailed chord symbols in the previous example to describe the extensions/alterations added with the double-4th shapes, experienced musicians will often use these voicings to upgrade basic major, minor, or dominant chord symbols on a chart (if the style and context permit).

In the previous example, we saw that it was possible to build double-4th shapes from the fourth/eleventh and the fifth of minor seventh chords. Here's a twelve-bar minor blues that uses these voicings on all of the minor seventh chords.

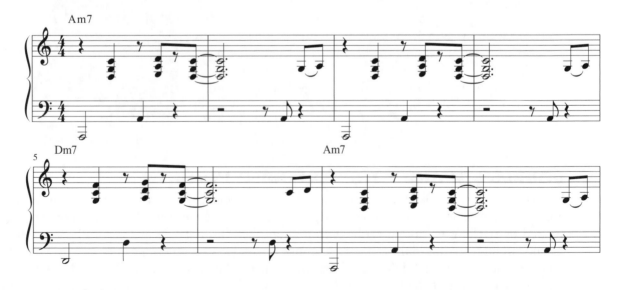

Next we'll see an example of double-4th shapes used in a modern rock song. Here's the piano intro from "Brick" by Ben Folds, which uses arpeggios of double-4th shapes and triads.

Brick

Words and Music by
Ben Folds and Darren Jessee

The arpeggiated chords in the treble clef of this example can be analyzed as follows:

Measures 1, 3, 5: The D chord is voiced with arpeggios of a D major triad, with a ninth (E) added during beat 3.

Measures 2, 4, 6: The G$_9^6$ chord is voiced with arpeggios of an inverted E–A–D double-4th shape, built from the sixth of the chord (refer to **Track 83**, measure 1, third voicing).

Measure 7: The Bm7 chord is voiced with arpeggios of a D major triad (built from the third of the chord), with an eleventh (E) added during beat 3.

Measure 8: The E7sus4 chord is voiced with an arpeggio of an inverted E–A–D double-4th shape, built from the root of the chord (refer to **Track 83**, measure 4, second voicing). The E7 chord is voiced with an arpeggio of the third, seventh, and root of the chord.

Next we'll take a look at an interesting type of voicing that I call a *7–3 extended voicing*. You'll recall that in Chapter 12 we introduced "7–3" voicings (the sevenths and thirds of the chords) into our discussion of the II–V–I progression (refer to **Track 56**). The seventh and third of a dominant chord (for example, the notes F and B of a G7 chord) form the interval of a *tritone* (augmented

4th/diminished 5th), and we can add a third note to this interval to extend the "7–3" voicing. Here is a series of "7–3" extended voicings of the G7 chord.

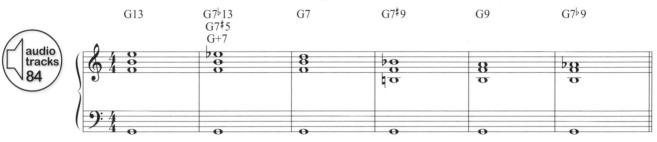

The bottom two notes of the treble-clef voicing in each case are the seventh and third of the G7 chord, and above these an extra note has been added. Note that the second measure has some alternate chord symbols provided. We saw in Chapter 16 that the "+" symbol meant that the fifth of the chord was sharped, and that the sharped fifth was equivalent to the flatted thirteenth. The three chord symbols in this measure are thus equivalent.

These additions to the basic dominant "7–3" voicing can be analyzed as follows:
- In measure 1, the thirteenth (E) has been added to the basic G7, creating a G13 chord.
- In measure 2, the sharped fifth or flatted thirteenth (E♭) has been added to the basic G7, creating a G7♯5, G7♭13, or G+7 chord.
- In measure 3, the fifth (D) has been added to the basic G7. As this is also a basic chord tone, the resulting chord is still a G7.
- In measure 4, the sharped ninth (spelled here as B♭, for consistency with the implied key of C minor) has been added to the basic G7, creating a G7♯9 chord.
- In measure 5, the ninth (A) has been added to the basic G7, creating a G9 chord.
- In measure 6, the flatted ninth (A♭) has been added to the basic G7, creating a G7♭9 chord.

Review Chapter 16 for more information on dominant chords and their extensions/alterations.

Now we'll look at a rhythmic pattern in a jazzy R&B style that uses some of these voicings.

The "7–3" extended voicings in this example are derived as follows:
- The ninth has been added above the seventh on the C9 in measures 1 and 4, and on the B♭9 in measure 4.
- The sharped fifth (♭13) has been added above the third on the A7♯5 in measure 1, and on the G7♯5 in measures 2 and 3.

- The sharped ninth has been added above the seventh on the D7#9 in measure 2, and on the B7#9 in measure 4.
- The thirteenth has been added above the third on the Ab13 in measure 3.

Next up is an example of "7–3" extended, double-4th, and upper-triad shapes used in a well-known jazz/rock song. Here's the keyboard intro to Steely Dan's "Deacon Blues."

Deacon Blues

Words and Music by
Walter Becker and Donald Fagen

The various upper-structure voicings in this example can be analyzed as follows:

Measures 1–5: The major seventh chords are all voiced by building minor triads from the third (Em/C, Dm/Bb, F#m/D, and Gm/Eb).

Measures 1–4: The chord on beat 3 of each measure is voiced as a double-4th shape, built from the ninth of the major chord placed over the third in the bass (refer to **Track 83**, measure 2).

Measures 5–6: The E7#9 chord is voiced by using a "7–3" extended shape ("3–7–#9"), which is then arpeggiated in successively higher octaves during measure 6.

"Deacon Blues" is one of Steely Dan's best-loved songs, and was included on their groundbreaking 1977 album *Aja*. Since the early 1970s, Steely Dan has been a vehicle for the jazz/rock songwriting and performing talents of Donald Fagen and Walter Becker, and the band is still active well into the 21st century. The *Aja* album featured some of the world's finest jazz and studio musicians of the period, including Larry Carlton (guitar), Victor Feldman (keyboards), Pete Christlieb (saxophone), and Bernard Purdie (drums).

Photo by Frank Ockenfels
Steely Dan

POLYCHORD VOICINGS

Finally we'll look at some *polychord voicings*, where we place one chord over another. This is an essential technique for jazz pianists and writers/arrangers. Although many chord and shape combinations are possible, here we're going to focus on a staple of the jazz setting: A triad or four-part chord, in the treble clef, over a double-4th or "7–3" extended shape in the bass clef. These polychord voicings work best when the lower shape is placed around the area of middle C. Here's another look at the first half of the jazz tune "Stella by Starlight," which we initially encountered in Chapter 18.

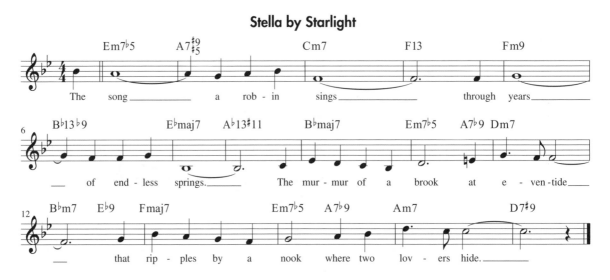

Now we'll apply some polychord voicings to the chords in this sixteen-measure section.

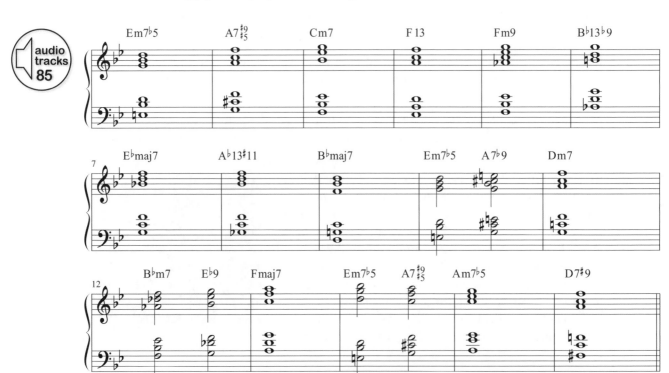

The polychord voicings used in the previous example can be analyzed as follows:

- The Em7♭5 chord in measures 1, 10, and 14 is voiced with a G minor triad in the treble clef (built from the third), over the "root–♭5–7" of the chord in the bass clef. This bass-clef voicing also looks like a "7–3" extended shape, except that it is built from the root of the minor seventh with flatted fifth chord rather than from the third of a dominant chord.

- The A7♯9♭5 chord in measures 2 and 14 is voiced with an F major triad in the treble clef (built from the sharped fifth), over a "7–3" extended shape ("7–3–♯5") in the bass clef.

- The Cm7 chord in measure 3 is voiced with an E♭ major triad in the treble clef (built from the third), over a double-4th shape (built from the fourth/eleventh) in the bass clef.

- The F13 chord in measure 4 is voiced with an F major triad in the treble clef (built from the root), over a "7–3" extended shape ("7–3–13") in the bass clef.

- The Fm9 chord in measure 5 is voiced with an A♭maj7 four-part chord in the treble clef (built from the third), over a double-4th shape (built from the root) in the bass clef.

- The B♭13♭9 chord in measure 6 is voiced with a G major triad in the treble clef (built from the thirteenth), over a "7–3" extended shape ("7–3–13") in the bass clef.

- The E♭maj7 chord in measure 7 is voiced with a B♭ major triad in the treble clef (built from the fifth), over a double-4th shape (built from the third) in the bass clef.

- The A♭13♯11 chord in measure 8 is voiced with a B♭ major triad in the treble clef (built from the ninth), over a "7–3" extended shape ("7–3–13") in the bass clef.

- The B♭maj7 chord in measure 9 is voiced with a B♭ major triad in the treble clef (built from the root), over a double-4th shape (built from the third) in the bass clef.

- The A7♭9 chord in measure 10 is voiced with a C♯°7 four-part chord in the treble clef (built from the third), over a "7–3" extended shape ("7–3–5") in the bass clef.

- The Dm7 chord in measure 11 is voiced with an F major triad in the treble clef (built from the third), over a double-4th shape (built from the fourth/eleventh) in the bass clef.

- The B♭m7 chord in measure 12 is voiced with a D♭ major triad in the treble clef (built from the third), over a double-4th shape (built from the fifth) in the bass clef. The E♭9 chord is voiced with an E♭ major triad in the treble clef (built from the root), over a "7–3" extended shape ("3–7–9") in the bass clef.

- The Fmaj7 chord in measure 13 is voiced with an F major triad in the treble clef (built from the root), over a double-4th shape (built from the third) in the bass clef.

- The Am7♭5 chord in measure 15 is voiced with a C minor triad in the treble clef (built from the third), over the "root–♭5–7" of the chord in the bass clef. This bass-clef voicing again looks like a "7–3" extended shape, similar to the Em7♭5 chord voicings in measures 1, 10, and 14.

- The D7♯9 chord in measure 16 is voiced with an F major triad in the treble clef (built from the sharped ninth), over a "7–3" extended shape ("3–7–♯9") in the bass clef.

Each of the dominant chords in the previous example is one of the chord types explained in Chapter 16. Review **Tracks 66–69** as necessary.

SECTION

5

Songs

Solfeggietto: C.P.E. Bach (piano)

Solfeggietto is a solo piano piece in C minor composed by C.P.E. Bach, the second surviving son of Johann Sebastian Bach. The melody moves back and forth between the treble and bass clefs, using arpeggios: For example, the Cm–G–Cm sequence in measures 1–2 and 3–4, and the Cm–Fm–B♭–E♭ sequence in measures 5–6.

Solfeggietto

By Carl Philipp Emanuel Bach

This Love: Maroon5 (piano)

"This Love" was the second single from the hit album *Songs about Jane* by the 21st-century rock band Maroon5. This transcription shows the actual piano part on the recording, together with the lead vocal part. Note the extensive use of upper triads and four-part chords in the piano part. The rhythmic feel is based around a straight-eighths rhythmic subdivision, with some added sixteenth-note syncopations.

This Love

Words and Music by
Adam Levine and Jesse Carmichael

Satin Doll: Duke Ellington (guitar)

"Satin Doll" is a swing-era jazz standard written by Duke Ellington (probably in collaboration with Billy Strayhorn). The guitar is the featured instrument on the CD track, and this transcription shows the guitar part in both regular notation and tablature. The guitar plays the melody on the first two choruses, before playing an improvised solo over the chord changes. On the last chorus, the guitar plays in a *chord melody* style (adding voicings below the melody).

Satin Doll
from SOPHISTICATED LADIES

Words by Johnny Mercer and Billy Strayhorn
Music by Duke Ellington

Money: Pink Floyd (bass)

"Money" is one of Pink Floyd's best-known songs, with the bass part providing the main thematic hook. This transcription shows the bass part from the recording in both regular notation and tablature. Most of the song uses an odd-time signature (7/4), which moves to 4/4 and 6/4 at the end of each verse. The time signature then switches to 4/4 for the guitar solo. The form of the tune is based on a minor blues (using the I, IV, and V chords): A modified thirteen-bar blues (using odd-time) for the verses, a 21-bar saxophone solo, and a more straight-ahead 24-bar blues for the guitar solo.

* Slur to 1st B note on repeats.

Additional Lyrics

2. Money, well, get back.
   I'm all right, Jack, keep your hands off of my stack.
   Money, it's a hit.
   Ah, don't give me that do-goody-good bullshit.
   I'm in the high-fidelity first-class traveling
   Set, and I think I need a Lear jet.

3. Money, it's a crime.
   Share it fairly, but don't take a slice of my pie.
   Money, so they say,
   Is the root of all evil today.
   But if you ask for a rise it's no surprise
   That they're giving none away.

Message in a Bottle: The Police (drums)

"Message in a Bottle" was a chart-topping single from the 1979 album *Reggatta de Blanc* by the Police. This transcription shows the drum part from the recording, together with the lyrics. The song has a straight-eighths rhythmic feel overall, with some sixteenth-note subdivisions added. Stewart Copeland is one of the most inventive drummers in rock music, and here the kick drum part is of particular interest, using upbeats during the intro, a more sparse part during the verses, a busier eighth-note pattern in the pre-chorus, a steady quarter-note pattern during the chorus, and so on.

Message in a Bottle

Music and Lyrics by Sting

Intro
Moderately fast ♩ = 150

Verse

1. Just a cast - a - way,___ an is - land lost___ at sea,___

___ oh.___ An - oth - er lone - ly day,___

no one here___ but me,___ oh.___ More

lone - li - ness___ than an - y man___ could bear.___

Res - cue me___ be - fore I fall___ in - to de - spair,___